Advanced Taxation (ATX-UK)
(Finance Act 2018)

**For June 2019 to March 2020
Examination Sittings**

Pocket Notes

British library cataloguing-in-publication data

A catalogue record for this book is available from the British Library.

Published by:
Kaplan Publishing UK
Unit 2 The Business Centre
Molly Millars Lane
Wokingham
Berkshire
RG41 2QZ

ISBN 978-1-78740-131-0

© Kaplan Financial Limited, 2018

Printed and bound in Great Britain.

Contents

KAPLAN PUBLIS

Preface

These Pocket Notes contain the key points you need to know for the exam, presented in a unique way that makes revision easy and effective.

Written by experienced lecturers and authors, these Pocket Notes break down content into manageable chunks to maximise your concentration.

Quality and accuracy are of the utmost importance to us so if you spot an error in any of our products, please send an email to mykaplanreporting@kaplan.com with full details, or follow the link to the feedback form in MyKaplan.

Our Quality Co-ordinator will work with our technical team to verify the error and take action to ensure it is corrected in future editions.

The exam

Section A (60%)

- Two compulsory case-study questions:

  Question 1: 35 marks

  Question 2: 25 marks

  There will also be 5 ethics marks and 4 professional skills marks available in this section.

Section B (40%)

- 2 compulsory 20-mark questions, covering both business and personal tax issues.

The entire syllabus can be tested in either section A or section B.

Candidates will be expected to undertake both calculation and narrative work. The questions will be scenario-based and may involve consideration of more than one tax, some elements of planning and the interaction of taxes.

The examination time is 3 hours and 15 minutes.

Topics which are not tested at TX and are new to ATX will be frequently examined. However, candidates will also need a thorough knowledge and understanding of the basic tax rules tested in the TX syllabus.

Exam focus

The examining team has stated that the ATX exam will concentrate on the application of tax rules and will require the demonstration of evaluation and explanation skills.

They will set questions involving:

- the interaction of taxes
- decision making within the facts of a given situation
- making choices in a given situation and evaluating the tax savings which can be made.

Questions in section A will be open ended and are likely to require presentation in the form of a report or letter.

Section B questions will be more structured in their requirements.

Aim of the paper

To apply relevant knowledge and skills and exercise professional judgement in providing relevant information and advice to individuals and businesses on the impact of the major taxes on financial decisions and situations.

Main capabilities

Understanding of the tax system through the study of more advanced topics within the taxes studied previously and the study of stamp taxes (A)

Impact of relevant taxes on various situations and courses of action, including the interaction of taxes (B)

Minimising and/or deferring tax liabilities by the use of standard tax planning measures (C)

Communication with clients, H M Revenue and Customs and other professionals in an appropriate manner (D)

The keys to success: ATX

Master the technical content

- Learn the rules, definitions and pro formas
- Practise questions to improve your ability to apply the techniques and perform the calculations
- Practise writing explanations of the rules to improve your understanding and written skills
- Be prepared to produce a report /letter / memorandum.

Provide advice and exercise judgement

– Higher skills

- Express yourself in clear, concise technical language.
- Apply common sense to the problem as well as your technical knowledge.
- Tailor your answer to the facts of the question and make references to the scenario given.
- Be prepared to express an opinion or draw a conclusion from the facts given – if the question asks for an opinion, give one.
- Be prepared to suggest improvements to a proposed strategy and to identify tax planning opportunities.
- When dealing with more than one tax, address each one separately.

1

Income tax – overview and investment income

In this chapter

- Income tax pro forma.
- Rates of income tax.
- Married couples and civil partners.
- Exempt income.
- Property income.
- Rent-a-room relief.
- Furnished holiday accommodation.
- Real estate investment trusts.

The computation of income tax is likely to feature throughout the examination.

Income from property is another key topic covered in this chapter.

It is also important to understand the marginal effect of transactions (i.e. the additional income tax payable as a result of receiving additional income, or the income tax savings where income is reduced).

The income tax computation is essential knowledge.

Use the following pro forma to gain easy marks on this aspect of the examination.

Income tax pro forma

Income tax computation – 2018/19

	£
Total income	x
Less: Reliefs	(x)
Net income	x
Less: Personal allowance	(x)
Taxable income	x

Income tax – analyse income

	Non-savings	Savings	Dividend
Basic rate band (first £34,500)	20%	20%	7.5%
Higher rate band (£34,501 – £150,000)	40%	40%	32.5%
Additional rate band (over £150,000)	45%	45%	38.1%

Income tax payable

	£
Total income tax (per rates)	x
Less: Tax reducers	(x)
Income tax liability	x
Less: Tax credits/PAYE	(x)
Payments on account	(x)
Income tax payable/(repayable)	x/(x)

Notes:

(1) If savings nil income falls into the first £5,000 of taxable income it is taxed at 0% (not 20%).

(2) A savings income nil rate band of £1,000/£500 is available to basic/higher rate taxpayers respectively – The savings income nil rate band is not available to additional rate taxpayers.

(3) All taxpayers are entitled to a £2,000 dividend nil rate band.

(4) Overseas income assessed under the remittance basis will be subject to income tax at the non-savings income rates. The savings and dividend nil rate bands and the lower rates applicable to dividends will not be available.

Key Point

Extend the basic rate and higher rate bands if a taxpayer makes payments into a personal pension scheme.

Exam focus

Section A questions
- Mirtoon
- Ziti
- Pippin

Section B questions
- Shuttelle
- Stella and Maris
- Kesme and Soba
- Cate and Ravi
- Traiste Ltd

Reliefs

- Interest on qualifying loans – paid gross
- Loss reliefs
- Maximum deduction from total income = greater of
  - £50,000
  - 25% x adjusted total income (ATI)
- Therefore the restriction will be £50,000 unless ATI exceeds £200,000.
- ATI is calculated as:

	£
Total income	X
Less: Gross PPCs	(X)
ATI	X

Exam focus

The maximum restriction is more likely to be examined in the context of loss relief (Chapter 13)

Personal allowance (PA)

- Available to all individuals
- £11,850 for 2018/19
- Deducted from net income to give taxable income
- Transferable amount £1,190 (see later)
- Lost if not used in the year

Exam focus

Exam kit questions on this area:

Section B questions

- Amy and Bex

Reduction of PA – higher rate taxpayers

- If Adjusted net income (ANI) > £100,000:
  - reduce PA by:
    50% × (ANI – £100,000)
- If ANI > £123,700:
  - no PA
- Effective rate of tax on income between £100,000 to £123,700: 60%
- ANI is calculated as:

	£
Net income per IT comp	x
Less: Gross gift aid	(x)
Less: Gross PPCs	(x)
ANI	x

Exam focus

Exam kit questions on this area:

Section B questions

- Tetra
- Shuttelle

Marriage Allowance

- A spouse or civil partner can elect to transfer a fixed amount of the PA to their spouse/civil partner.
- This is known as the marriage allowance (MA).
- Neither spouse/civil partner may be a higher or additional rate taxpayer.

Method:

- The fixed amount of PA to transfer:
  = £1,190 for 2018/19.
- There is no provision for transferring less than this amount.
- Relief is given by reducing the recipient's income tax liability by a maximum of £238 (i.e. £1,190 x 20% BR income tax).

Tax reducers

- EIS, SEIS and VCT relief
  = 30%/50%/30%

- DTR = Lower of UK and overseas tax

Rates of income tax

- Income tax rate bands apply to the different types of income in the following order:

  1. non-savings income

  2. savings income

  3. dividend income

- To maximise tax relief in most cases offset PA and reliefs against income in the same order as above.

- In some circumstances it is beneficial to offset the PA in a different order e.g. offset against dividend income first to avoid wasting the savings starting rate o nil rate band.

Income

Non-savings income:

- Employment income
- Trading income
- Property income
- Pension income
- Trust income: discretionary, or property income from an IIP trust.

Savings income:

- Interest received net of (20%) tax: interest from an IIP trust, unquoted loan stock issued by UK resident companies.
- Interest received gross: NS&I accounts, gilts, treasury stock, exchequer stock, quoted loan stock issued by UK resident companies, bank and building societies.

Dividend income:

- This includes overseas dividends for all UK resident individuals.

Married couples and civil partners

Joint income

- Applies to married couples and civil partnerships.
- The income arising from assets (except shares in close companies) held jointly by husband and wife is normally split 50:50.
- An election is available to split the income according to beneficial ownership.
- The election cannot be made for joint bank or building society accounts.

Parental dispositions

- Income earned by a child from a parental disposition = taxed on the parent if the gross income received in the tax year exceeds £100 p.a.

Exempt income

- Interest on:
  - NS&I savings certificates
  - Save As You Earn (SAYE) share save accounts
  - Repayment interest (interest on tax repayments)
- Dividends received on shares from venture capital trusts (VCTs).
- Scholarships and educational grants.
- Prizes and winnings (i.e. premium bonds, betting).
- Statutory redundancy pay and the first £30,000 of compensation received for loss of employment.
- Certain state benefits (Child benefit, Universal credit).

- Income from individual savings accounts (ISAs).
- On death of a spouse/civil partner:
  - value of ISAs held at death = available as additional ISA allowance for surviving spouse/civil partner.

Property income

- Taxes income from land and property.
- Taxable income calculated using trading income rules; wholly and exclusively test.
- Assessed on a cash basis.
- Accruals basis is compulsory if gross annual rent >£150,000 or can elect to use accruals basis.
- Taxed as other income at:
  - 20%, 40% or 45%.
- Additional points re expenses:
  - interest paid = allowable deduction for individuals subject to special rules (see below)
  - replacement furniture relief for the cost of replacing furnishings

- Property income losses
- for individuals, can only be carried forward against future UK property income.

Pro forma – property income

	£
Rent received in the tax year	X
Plus: Rental income portion of short lease premiums received in tax year (see below)	A
Less: Allowable expenses	(X)
Profit / (loss)	X/(X)

Financing costs

- Tax relief restricted to basic rate.
- Applies to finance costs relating to loans to buy or improve residential property.
- Being phased in gradually.
- For 2018/19:
  - 50% of finance costs deductible from property income.
  - Tax relief for remaining 50% given at basic rate (20%) by deduction from income tax liability.
- Note: No restrictions for:
  - companies
  - loans relating to furnished holiday accommodation
  - loans relating to non-residential properites.

Premium for granting short leases only

Income element is calculated as:

	£
Premium	x
Less: 2% x premium x (n – 1)	(x)
Income element	A

Alternative calculation:

$$A = \text{Premium} \times \frac{51 - n}{50}$$

Where n = no. of years of lease

Rent-a-room relief

- Furnished room in a main domestic residence.
- Gross rents ≤ £7,500
  - exempt, unless elect for loss.
- Gross rents > £7,500
  - normal property income calculation
  - unless elect for excess over £7,500 to be taxed (with no deduction for expenses).

Exam focus

Exam kit questions on this area:

Section B questions

- Kesme and Soba

Furnished holiday accommodation (FHA)

- Assessed as property income but:
  - treat as arising from a single and separate trade.
- Advantages:
  - business asset for CGT rollover relief, gift relief and entrepreneurs' relief
  - relevant earnings for pensions relief
  - finance costs fully deductible
  - deduction available for all P&M, including furniture, if using cash basis
  - capital allowances available for P&M, including furniture, if using accruals basis
  - 100% of finance costs deductible from FHA income.

- Losses:
  - can only be set against profits from the same FHA business
  - UK FHA losses can only be set against UK FHA profits
  - EEA FHA losses can only be set against EEA FHA profits
  - firstly offset in the same year
  - then carry forward.
- Conditions:
  - situated in UK or EEA
  - let furnished on commercial basis
  - available to let $\geqslant$ 210 days/tax year
  - actually let $\geqslant$ 105 days/tax year
  - if own more than one property, averaging is available to satisfy the 105 day rule
  - not let for periods of 'long term occupation' (occupied by same person > 31 consecutive days) in excess of 155 days in a 12 month period.

Exam focus

Exam kit questions on this area:

Section B questions

- Monisha and Horner

Real estate investment trusts (REITs)

- Quoted property investment trust.
- Dividends received by individual from REIT:
  - treated as property income
  - received net of 20% tax.

2

Employment income
– income tax and national insurance

In this chapter

- Employment income – pro forma.
- Benefits summary.
- Vehicle benefits.
- Living accommodation.
- Beneficial loans.
- Use of assets.
- Gift of assets.
- Share options – tax treatment.
- Tax advantaged schemes.
- Lump sum payments.
- National insurance.

Employment is a particularly important area.

Skills required may vary from performing the basic calculation of employee benefits to higher skills. For example, making decisions between whether an employee should accept a company car or run their own car and take a cash alternative from the business instead.

You may also be required to express an opinion on whether an individual, given a particular scenario, is likely to be treated as self-employed or as an employee.

Employment income – pro forma

	£	£
Salary		x
Bonus/Commission		x
Benefits		x
Gross earnings		x
Less: Allowable expenses (See overleaf)		(x)
Add: Redundancy payment	x	
Less: Exempt portion (First £30,000 of non-contractual redundancy is tax free)	(x)	
		x
Employment income		x

Exam kit questions on this area:

Section A questions

- Florina, Kanzi and Winston

Section B questions

- Morice and Babine plc
- Jerome and Tricycle ltd
- Shuttelle
- Cate and Ravi
- Methley Ltd
- Traiste Ltd
- Damiana plc
- Jessica

Allowable expenses

- Contributions to employers registered occupational pension scheme.
- Subscriptions to professional bodies.
- Charitable donations under a payroll deduction scheme.
- Travel, subsistence and entertaining incurred wholly, exclusively and necessarily in the performance of the office or employment (see Note).
- Cost of partnership shares acquired in a share incentive plan (SIP).
- Deficit on mileage allowance (AMAP).

Note: Travel and related expenses

- Not travel from home to permanent workplace.
- Travel from home to a temporary workplace is allowed if the placement is expected to last less than 2 years.

Benefits summary

Taxable benefits	Exempt benefits
General rule: Assessed on cost to employer (marginal cost if 'in house' benefit) **Special rules**: Non-cash vouchers – cost to employer Accommodation – see below Company cars/vans/fuel Beneficial loans Gift and use of assets Accommodation – See below	• Job-related accommodation • Subsidised canteen (unless part of salary sacrifice scheme) • Up to £4 per week towards additional household costs where the employee works from home • Occupational pension contributions • Workplace parking • Relocation expenses ≤ £8,000 • Overnight subsistence • Mobile phone (one) • Workplace nurseries • Annual party ≤ £150 per person per annum • Eye care tests • Cheap loans ≤ £10,000 • AMAPs • Recommended medical treatment assisting return to work (up to £500 per employee per tax year)

Exam focus

Points frequently examined:

- employee contributions

  - deduct amounts paid in tax year from benefit

  - but note special rules for car: capital contributions (max £5,000) and fuel contributions (not allowable)

- where the benefit is wholly and exclusive for employment

  - calculate benefit and deduct expense claim

- benefits not available for part of year

  - time apportion.

Approved mileage allowance payments (AMAPs)

If employee uses own car, van, motorcycle or bicycle for business purposes:

AMAPs = tax free

If mileage allowance received > AMAP:

Excess = taxable benefit

If mileage allowance received < AMAP:

Shortfall = allowable deduction from employment income

Passenger payments (if provided) for taking colleagues on same business trip:

- tax free if up to statutory limit (5p per passenger)
- no deduction for a shortfall.

Exam focus

- The AMAP rates for cars and vans will be provided in the tax rates and allowances (but not the passenger or other rates).

Exam focus

Exam kit questions on this area:

Section B questions

- Hyssop Ltd
- Morice and Babine plc
- Jerome and Tricycle Ltd
- Shuttelle
- Spike
- Methley Ltd

Vehicle benefits

Where employer provides vehicle used for private purposes by employee.

VEHICLE BENEFITS

Car benefit

Basic car benefit:

List price $\times$ % $\times \frac{n}{12}$

- list price, including extras
- employee capital contribution deductible (max £5,000)
- benefit reduced if unavailable > 30 days
- benefit includes all running costs except private fuel
- n = number of months car available

Private fuel

$£23,400 \times \% \times \frac{n}{12}$

- % based on car percentage
- Employee contributions ignored unless reimburses private fuel in full

Van benefit

- £3,350 p.a. for use of van
- £633 p.a. for private fuel
- Time apportion if unavailable > 30 days

Appropriate %

The percentage used to calculate the car benefit depends on CO_2 emissions.

Emission rate per kilometre travelled ('Base level')	Percentage
95 grams (given in exam)	20% petrol
Increased by 1% for every extra 5 grams emitted	(max 37%)
4% supplement for diesel engines	(max 37%)

Low emission car reduced rates:

CO_2 emission rate ≤ 50 g/km:	13% (petrol) or 17% (diesel)
CO_2 emissions 51-75 g/km:	16% (petrol) or 20% (diesel)
CO_2 emissions 76-94 g/km:	19% (petrol) or 23% (diesel)

Living accommodation

Benefit	Amount taxable	Job-related accommodation
Basic charge	Higher of: • Annual value • Rent paid by employer	Exempt
Expensive accommodation charge (where employer owns property and cost is > £75,000)	(Cost – £75,000) × ORI ORI = official rate of interest (provided in the exam)	Exempt
Ancillary services: • Use of furniture	20% x market value when first provided	Same as for non-job related accommodation except: Maximum total benefit restricted to 10% of other employment income
• Living expenses (e.g. heating, electricity, decorating)	Cost to employer	
• Council tax	Cost to employer	No charge

- Where the employer rents the accommodation there can never be an expensive accommodation charge.

- For the expensive accommodation charge:

  Cost = Acquisition cost of the property **plus** capital improvements up to the **start** of the tax year.

  If the property is occupied by the employee more than 6 years after it was acquired by the employer:

  - substitute the acquisition cost with the market value at the date the property was first occupied.

Job-related accommodation

Definition

Accommodation which is:

- necessary for proper performance of employee's duties, or

- provided for the better performance of duties and it is customary to provide such accommodation, or

- provided as part of special security arrangements because of a specific threat to the employee's security.

Exam focus

Exam kit questions on this area:

Section B questions

- Shuttelle

Beneficial loans

Where an interest free/subsidised loan made to employee:

	£
Capital (see below)	
x official rate of interest (ORI)	X
Less: Interest actually paid	(X)
Taxable benefit	X

- ORI = 2.5% for June 2019 to March 2020 exam sittings (given in tax tables)

- Two methods of calculation of capital:

  - Average method:

    $$\frac{\text{Opening balance} + \text{Closing balance}}{2} = \text{average capital}$$

  - Precise method:
    calculated each month on balance outstanding

- Either taxpayer or HMRC can elect for precise method to be used

Exceptions

- No benefit if:

  - total loans outstanding at any time the tax year is ≤ £10,000, or

  - loans made on ordinary commercial terms (i.e. same terms as to public)

Exam focus

- The benefit should be calculated using both methods in the examination unless the questions states otherwise.

Use of assets

- Benefit:

  20% × MV when first made available

- 20% rule does not apply to private use of cars, vans and accommodation provided by employer.

Gift of assets

New asset:

Benefit = cost to employer.

Used asset:

- Benefit is greater of:

  Method 1

	£
– Market value at time of transfer	X
Less: Amount paid by employee	(X)
	X

  and

  Method 2

– Market value when first used	X
Less: Amount charged as benefit over period of use	(X)
Less: Amount paid by employee	(X)
	X

- These rules do not apply to transfer of:

  - a used car or van

  - bicycles provided for work.

  The benefit in this instance
  = Method 1

Share options – tax treatment

	Non-tax advantaged (unapproved)	**Tax advantaged (approved)**
Grant of option	No tax	No tax

Exercise of options (i.e. buy shares)	Income tax and NIC
	Collected under PAYE immediately
	Employment income charge:
	
	                           £
	MV @ exercise date x
	Less:
	  Cost of option (x)
	  Cost of shares (x)
	Employment income charge x
		No tax

Sale of shares	CGT £ Proceeds x Less: Cost of shares (x) Chargeable gain x Cost of shares = MV when exercised	CGT £ Proceeds x Less: Cost of shares (x) Chargeable gain x Cost of shares = Exercise price

Notes

(1) Class 1A NIC will be payable by the employer:

- unless the shares are quoted,
- in which case class 1 will apply, which means the employee will also be liable.

(2) The gain is taxed at 0%, 10%, or 20% depending on the availability of the AEA, entrepreneurs' relief and level of taxable income.

(3) Entrepreneurs' relief will only be available if:

- the employee owns at least 5% shareholding of the company
- for the 12 months prior to sale.

Except for EMI shares, where:

- the 12 months ownership commences at the date the option is granted, and
- there is no 5% holding requirement.

Exam focus

Exam kit questions on this area:

Section B questions

- Spike
- Damiana plc

Tax advantaged schemes

Tax advantaged share option schemes

	CSOP	EMI	SAYE
Participation	Employer chooses	Employer chooses	All employees
Maximum value	£30,000 per employee	£250,000 per employee Scheme max £3m	£500 per month
Exercise period	3 – 10 years	Up to 10 years	3 or 5 years
Issue price	MV	Issue at MV to avoid IT charge	Not < 80% of MV
Base cost of shares for CGT	Price paid	Price paid plus discount taxed as income on exercise (if any)	Price paid
Other	If own > 30% of company = excluded from the scheme	Gross assets ≤ £30m Employees < 250 ER period of ownership runs from date of grant (not date shares acquired) and no need to own ≥ 5% of OSC	

Share incentive plan (SIP)

Participation	All employees
Awarded free shares	Max £3,600 per year
Purchase partnership shares	Max = lower of: • £1,800, and • 10% salary Cost = allowable deduction against employment income
Awarded matching shares	Max 2 per partnership share
Dividends	Tax free if invested in further shares

Holding period	• 5 years – IT and NIC free
	• If 3-5 years IT and NIC on lower of:
	  – initial value of the shares
	  – Value of the date of withdrawal
	• If 3 years
	  IT and NIC on value of the shares at the time when they cease to be held in the plan

Base cost of shares	MV when removed from plan

Exam focus

In the examination you may be required to recommend a suitable tax advantaged share scheme based on the facts in a particular situation.

Use the following factors to assist in deciding the most appropriate option:

- participants – open to all/selective scheme
- share award vs share option scheme
- financial limits – amount to be awarded
- size of company – EMI only available to smaller companies
- holding period for shares/options.

Exam focus

Exam kit questions on this area:
Section B questions

- Morice and Babine plc
- Klubb plc
- Methley Ltd

Lump sum payments

- generally associated with termination.
- but may be used as an incentive to attract an employee.

Three types:

Wholly exempt	Fully taxable	First £30,000 exempt
• Payments for death, injury and disability • Statutory redundancy pay • Approved lump sum on retirement	• Pay in lieu of notice • Reward for past or future services	• Genuine ex-gratia payments for loss of office (see below)

Termination payments on loss of office

- If contractual = taxable
- If non-contractual / ex-gratia
  = first £30,000 exempt
  - £30,000 includes statutory redundancy pay
- Restrictive covenants (i.e. restraint of trade) = fully taxable.

Taxable amounts

- Assessed in year of receipt
- Paid before P45 = Paid net of PAYE
- Paid after P45 = Paid net of marginal rate income tax
- Taxed as top slice of income (after dividends).

Exam focus

Exam kit questions on this area:
Section B questions

- Tetra
- Pita plc
- Amy and Bex
- Traiste Ltd
- Jessica

National insurance

Employees

Employee class 1

- Employees pay class 1 NICs on their 'cash earnings'.
- Cash earnings includes:
  - any remuneration derived from employment and paid in money
  - vouchers exchangeable for cash or goods
  - reimbursement of cost of travel between home and work.
- Cash earnings does not include:
  - exempt employment benefits
  - most non-cash benefits
  - reimbursement of business expenses.
  - mileage allowance ≤ 45p per mile.
- Payable by all employees
  - aged 16 to state pension age.

- Payable at 12% on earnings between £8,424 and £46,350.
- Payable at 2% on earnings above £46,350.
- Contributions are collected by the employer through the PAYE scheme.

Employers

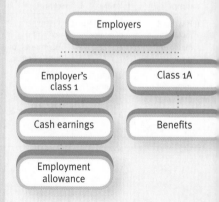

Employer's class 1

- Cost borne by employer.
- Allowable trading expense for tax purposes.
- Rate of 13.8% on earnings over £8,424 per annum.
- Paid on 'cash earnings', as for employee class 1.
- Paid in respect of employees aged ≥ 16.
- Employment allowance available.
- Payable with employee class 1 contributions through PAYE system.
- Payable on 22nd of the next month (electronic payments), or 19th of the next month if not paid electronically.

Employment allowance

- Up to £3,000 p.a. allowance.
- Deducted from employer's class 1 NICs only.
- Not available where a director is the company's only employee.
- Claimed though the PAYE system.

Class 1A

- Payable by the employer only.
- Rate of 13.8% on taxable benefits provided to the employee.
- Payable by 22 July following the tax year if paid electronically) or 19 July (if not paid electronically).

3

Relief for pensions

In this chapter

- Pensions – overview.
- Types of registered pension schemes.
- Tax relief.
- Annual allowance.
- Lifetime allowance.
- Benefits on retirement.

Individuals investing in a registered pension scheme can reduce their income tax liability at their highest marginal rate in the tax year in which they make the investment.

Questions may require you to:

- provide information regarding the rules about the maximum amount a person is permitted to invest in their pension scheme

- advise a client as to how much tax they can save if they invest in a registered pension scheme, and/or

- advise a client as to the maximum amount they should invest in a particular tax year in order to maximise their tax relief.

Pensions – overview

- Tax relief available for contributions by under 75 year olds into HMRC registered pension schemes.

- Scheme must satisfy conditions.

Types of registered pension schemes

HMRC registered pension schemes

Employed

Self employed

Pensionable employment

Non-pensionable employment

Occupational Pension Plan (OPP)

Personal Pension Plan (PPP)

Tax relief

Tax relief available for contributions into HMRC registered pensions of up to:

Lower of:

(a) Total gross contributions paid

(b) Maximum amount = Higher of:

   (i) £3,600
   (ii) 100% x (relevant earnings).

Relevant earnings = trading profits,
employment income,
FHA income.

Exam focus

Exam kit questions on this area:
Section B questions

- Tetra
- Shuttelle
- Stella and Maris
- Jessica

Method of relief

Employee contributions

OPP	Allowable deduction against employment income
PPP	Basic rate relief
	• at source
	Higher rate / additional rate relief
	• extend basic rate band / higher rate band

Employer contributions

- tax allowable against business profits
- exempt benefit for individual
- taken into account when calculating total contributions to be compared with the annual allowance (AA).

Annual allowance (AA)

- Where total contributions paid into pension schemes > the current year AA plus unused AA b/f:
  - a tax charge arises on the excess.
- The tax charge is:
  - taxed as the individual's top slice of income
  - paid through the self-assessment system.

In the examination:

- tax the excess last (i.e. after dividends) at non-savings rates.

- Unused AA b/f from the **previous three tax years** is taken into account:
  - can only be c/f if the individual was a member of a registered pension scheme for that tax year.
- Order of utilisation:
  - current year AA is used first
  - then earlier three years unused amount, on a FIFO basis.

Exam kit questions on this area:

Section B questions

- Shuttelle
- Stella and Maris
- Sabrina and Adam
- Jessica

Restriction of annual allowance – high income individuals

- The annual allowance is gradually reduced for individuals with high income.
- The restriction applies to individuals with a 'threshold income' exceeding £110,000 and 'adjusted income' exceeding £150,000.
- The annual allowance is reduced by: (Adjusted income – £150,000) × 50%.
- The maximum reduction to the annual allowance is £30,000, meaning the minimum annual allowance is £10,000.

Threshold income

	£
Net income (from the income tax computation)	X
Less: Individual's **gross personal pension** contributions	(X)
Threshold income	X

Adjusted income

	£
Net income (from the income tax computation)	X
Plus: Individual's **employee's occupational pension** contributions	X
Employer's contributions into any scheme for that individual	X
Adjusted income	X

If threshold income ≤ £110,000	The annual allowance for the tax year is £40,000 (no restriction).
If threshold income > £110,000 and adjusted income ≤ £150,000:	
If threshold income is > £110,000 and adjusted income > £150,000:	The annual allowance for the tax year must be reduced by (adjusted income – £150,000) x 50%.

Lifetime allowance (LA)

- LA = Total pension value that can obtain tax relief.
- LA can not exceed £1,030,000.
- Considered when individual becomes entitled to take his pension/lump sum on retirement.
- If the value of the pension fund at the time exceeds the LA: an additional charge arises.

Benefits on retirement

Pension fund grows tax-free

- Exempt income tax.
- Exempt capital gains tax.

Commencement of benefits

- Aged 55.
- Can continue to work and draw a pension.

Tax free lump sum

- Maximum = 25% of lower of:
  - (1) value of fund
  - (2) lifetime allowance (LA).
- The balance of the fund can be withdrawn at any time.
- Withdrawals from the balance are subject to income tax at normal rates (20%, 40% or 45%).

If value of fund > LA:

- Income tax charge on excess
  - at 25% if used to purchase a pension
  - at 55% if taken as a lump sum.

Pension income

- Pension income = taxable earned income.
- On death – pension income and/or lump sums for dependants may be made.

4

Capital gains tax – introduction

In this chapter

- Scope of CGT.
- CGT computation procedure – individuals.
- Pro forma CGT computation.
- Chargeable gain computation – individuals.
- Part disposals.
- Chattels.
- Assignment of leases.
- Assets lost or destroyed.
- Asset damaged.
- Capital losses.
- Connected persons.
- Married couples and civil partners.

Evaluation of capital gains and losses is likely to feature heavily in the examination.

Questions are likely to feature both computational and planning aspects.

This chapter provides the tools to enable you to deal with the computational aspects of different scenarios.

Scope of CGT

- A chargeable gain arises when:
  - a chargeable disposal is made
  - by a chargeable person
  - of a chargeable asset.
- Companies
  - pay corporation tax.
- Individuals
  - pay capital gains tax.

Scope of CGT

Chargeable persons

- individual
- company
- trustee
- partners in a partnership

Chargeable assets

- all assets unless specifically exempt

Chargeable disposals

- sale/gift of whole/part of asset
- loss/destruction of asset
- compensation for damage
- capital sums received re surrender of rights

Exempt assets

- gains – no CGT
- losses – no relief
- examples:
  - qualifying corporate bonds (QCBs) owned by individuals
  - gilts
  - trading inventory
  - receivables
  - equity ISA investments
  - cash
  - endowment policy proceeds
  - motor cars
  - wasting chattels (e.g. horses, boats)
  - shares in VCT

Exempt disposals

- trading disposal
- transfers on death
- gifts to charity

CGT computation procedure – individuals

Compute the CGT payable by an individual for a tax year as follows:

(1) Calculate the chargeable gains / allowable losses on the disposal of each chargeable asset separately

(2) Consider availability of any CGT reliefs (Chapter 6)

(3) Calculate the net chargeable gains arising in the tax year

= (chargeable gains less allowable losses)

(4) Deduct capital losses brought forward

(5) Deduct the annual exempt amount (AEA) = taxable gains

(6) Calculate the CGT payable at 10% and/ or 20% depending on the availability of entrepreneurs' relief (ER) and level of taxable income (18%/28% for residential property).

Pro forma CGT computation

	£
Net chargeable gains for tax year (after specific reliefs)	X
Less: Capital losses b/f	(X)
	X
Less: AEA (2018/19)	(11,700)
Taxable gains	X
CGT payable (at appropriate rate)	X

Due date   31 January 2020
(31 January after end of tax year)

Chargeable gain computation – individuals

The following pro forma can be used as the basic layout for the computation of the chargeable gain/allowable loss arising on each disposal by an individual.

Elements of the pro forma are computed differently for specific assets (e.g. part disposals). The approach to take for assets with additional rules is shown on the subsequent pages.

	£
Consideration (a), (b)	X
Less: Incidental costs of sale (c)	(X)
Net disposal proceeds	X
Less: Allowable expenditure	
– acquisition cost (d)	(X)
– incidental costs of acquisition (c)	(X)
– enhancement expenditure	(X)
Chargeable gain/loss	X/(X)

If a chargeable gain arises:

Chargeable gain before reliefs	X
Less: CGT reliefs (e)	(X)
Chargeable gain after reliefs	X

If an allowable loss arises:

Deduct any capital losses for the year from chargeable gains and include the net chargeable gains in the pro forma CGT payable computation.

Notes

(a) Disposal proceeds or market value (MV).

(b) Date of disposal:
date of contract/date conditions satisfied
for conditional contracts.

(c) Legal expenses, valuation fees,
advertising costs, stamp duty,
auctioneer's fees.

(d) Cost/MV/probate value.

(e) Gift relief, rollover relief, incorporation
relief, PPR and letting relief, EIS/SEIS
relief.

(f) The gain is aggregated with other gains
and losses and taxed at 10%, or 20%
depending on the AEA, ER and the level
of taxable income. (18% or 28% for
residential property gains)

KAPLAN PUBLIS

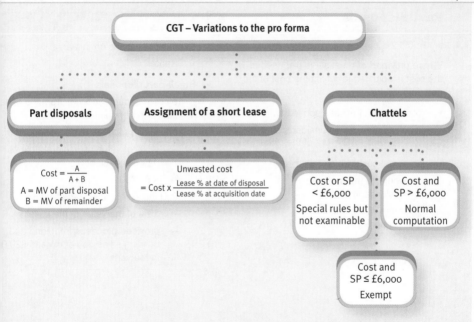

CGT – Variations to the pro forma

Part disposals

$$\text{Cost} = \frac{A}{A + B}$$
A = MV of part disposal
B = MV of remainder

Assignment of a short lease

Unwasted cost
$$= \text{Cost} \times \frac{\text{Lease \% at date of disposal}}{\text{Lease \% at acquisition date}}$$

Chattels

Cost or SP
< £6,000
Special rules but
not examinable

Cost and
SP > £6,000
Normal
computation

Cost and
SP ≤ £6,000
Exempt

Part disposals

Where only part of an asset is disposed of the cost is adjusted to reflect the cost of the part sold.

- Cost of part of asset disposed of:

  $\text{Cost} \times \dfrac{A}{A + B}$ 　　A = consideration
  　　　　　　　　B = MV of the remainder

- incidental costs which relate:

  - wholly to the part sold
    = fully deductible

  - to the whole assest
    = apportioned as above (i.e. A/A+B)

Exam kit questions on this area:

- Kantar

Small part disposals

- elect to deduct proceeds from the base cost of part retained

- applies if proceeds of part disposed of:

  - ≤ 5% of value of whole at date of part disposal, or

  - ≤ £3,000

- for land and buildings the limit is:

  - 20% of the value of the asset,

  - provided proceeds from land and building sales do not exceed £20,0● in the year.

Chattels

Tangible movable property
(e.g. painting, jewellery, racehorse, boat,
caravan).

Wasting chattels:

- expected life ≤ 50 years
  (e.g. racehorse, boat, caravan)
- exempt from CGT unless plant and
  machinery on which capital allowances
  available.

Non-wasting chattels:

- expected life > 50 years
  (e.g. antiques, painting)
- subject to £6,000 rule but special rules
  not examinable.

Assignment of leases

Long lease (i.e. > 50 years)	**Short lease** (i.e. ≤ 50 years)
• subject to normal CGT computation	• subject to special CGT computation • cost adjusted to reflect depreciating nature of the asset: Allowable cost × $\dfrac{\text{Percentage for remaining life on disposal}}{\text{Percentage for remaining life on acquisition}}$ The % will be provided in the examination

Exam focus

Exam kit questions on this area:

Section B questions:

Assets lost or destroyed

Asset damaged

Asset damaged

No insurance proceeds

Insurance proceeds received

No disposal

Not used in restoration

Used in restoration

Normal part disposal computation:
A/(A+B) where
A = Insurance received
B = Value of damaged asset

Part disposal **unless** 'rollover' election made to deduct proceeds from cost of restored asset on a subsequent disposal

 Exam focus

Exam kit questions in this area:

Section B questions:

- Eric

KAPLAN PUBLI

- Ash

Capital losses

- Current year losses:
  - must be offset against gains if possible
  - cannot be restricted to preserve the AEA
  - carry forward remaining losses.
- Brought forward losses:
  - offset after current year losses
  - but net chargeable gains must not be reduced below the AEA.
- Losses in the year of death:
  - can be carried back 3 years
  - LIFO basis

- can restrict to preserve AEA.

Connected persons

- Consideration for disposal = market value.
- Loss on disposal can only be offset against gains on disposals to the same connected person.

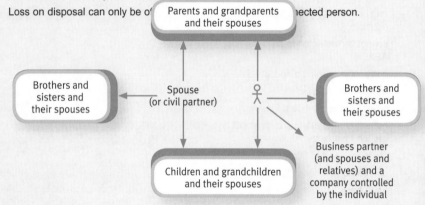

Civil partner and their relatives (as above) are also connected persons.

Married couples and civil partners

Scenarios involving married couples / civil partners are likely to be examined.

It is important that you know how to deal with transactions between spouses / civil partners and also to be able to suggest simple tax planning opportunities to enable them to minimise their total tax liabilities (see Chapter 12).

Exam kit questions on this area:

Section B questions:

- Monisha and Horner

For CGT purposes, spouse / civil partner transfers are treated as follows:

- The connected persons rules are overridden.

- Spouse or civil partner transfers:

  - take place at no gain/no loss

  - regardless of any actual consideration which may have been received.

- These rules only apply whilst the couple are living together (i.e. not separated).

- The transferor is deemed to dispose of the asset at its acquisition cost

  - i.e. the spouse/civil partner takes over the asset at its original cost.

5

Capital gains tax – shares and securities

In this chapter

- Share valuation rules.
- Matching rules – individuals.
- The share pool.
- Sale of rights (nil paid).
- Takeovers and mergers.
- QCBs and government securities.
- Liquidations.
- Losses on unquoted shares.

Share valuation rules

Transaction:	Consideration:
Sale	Sale proceeds
Gift	Market value
Transfer to a connected person	Market value

Market value of quoted shares:

Value = the mid- price quoted on the Stock Exchange

- i.e. the average of the lowest and highest prices on the disposal date.

Unquoted shares

- No readily available price
  – professional valuation required.
- In the exam the value will be given.

Matching rules – individuals

Apply where an individual has made more than one purchase of shares of the same class in the same company.

Disposals matched with:

1. Acquisitions on same day.

2. Acquisitions in the next 30 days (FIFO basis).

3. The share pool (shares acquired before the date of disposal are pooled together)

Exam focus

For the ATX examination, a thorough understanding of the basic share identification rules is required.

Disposal of shares by individuals

| Share pool | 30 days |

Date of disposal

Order of matching:

(3) (1) (2)

Method to calculate gain:

Step 1 Determine the sale proceeds per share.

Step 2 Identify the date the shares are purchased and using the matching rules allocate the disposal to the time periods above.

Step 3 Calculate the gains / losses arising on each matching rule.

The share pool

- The share pool contains shares in the same company, of the same class, purchased before the date of a disposal.

- It contains the amalgamated cost of shares acquired.

- The cost of shares disposed of is calculated as a proportion of the number of shares removed from the pool.

- If an individual disposes of shares:
  - in his personal trading company, and
  - is also an employee of that company:

  Entrepreneurs' relief (ER) is available (see Chapter 6).

Bonus issues

Distribution of free shares to shareholders based on their existing shareholding.

For CGT purposes bonus issues are treated as follows:

- The bonus shares are not treated as a separate holding of shares.
- The shares are treated as acquired on the same day as the original shares to which they relate.
- Therefore, the number of bonus shares are included in the share pool but at nil cost.

Rights issues

Offer of new shares to existing shareholders in proportion to their existing shareholding, usually at a price below the market price.

For CGT purposes rights issues are treated as follows:

- The rights shares are not treated as a separate holding of shares.
- The shares are treated as acquired on the same day as the original shares to which they relate.
- Therefore, the number of rights shares are included in the share pool, and the cost in the cost column in the same way as a normal purchase.

Sale of rights (nil paid)

Sales of rights (nil paid) = where shareholder does not take up rights issue and sells the 'right to buy' more shares.

The treatment of a 'sale of rights nil paid' for CGT purposes depends on the amount of sale proceeds (SP) received as follows:

If SP received are:	(i) > 5% of the value of the shares on which the rights are offered, **and** (ii) > £3,000.	(i) ⩽ 5% of the value of the shares on which the rights are offered, **or** (ii) ⩽ £3,000 if higher.
CGT treatment:	• deemed part disposal of original shares held. • normal part disposal computation required Where A = SP received B = MV of shares on which the rights are offered	• no chargeable disposal at the time of the sale of rights nil paid. • SP received are deducted from the cost of the original shares.

Takeovers and mergers

- Company (B) acquires shares in another company (A) by issuing shares to A's shareholders.

- 'Paper for paper'/'share for share' transaction = not a CGT disposal by A's shareholders.
  The new shares in B 'stand in shoes' of old A shares (i.e. take on the cost and acquisition date of A shares)

- Conditions:

  - clearance required from HMRC

  - B acquires > 25% of A's ordinary share capital (or a majority of the voting power of A)

  - the exchange is for bona fide commercial reasons and main purpose not the avoidance of tax.

With a share for share exchange, it is possible that:

- the old shares would qualify for ER if it were treated as a disposal

- but the new company is not the shareholder's personal trading company and so the later disposal of its shares would not qualify for relief.

However, the individual shareholder can:

- elect for the event to be treated as a disposal for CGT purposes, in which case the gain is taxed at 0%, 10%, or 20% depending on the availability of the AEA, ER, IR and level of taxable income.

If shares are sold for a mixture of cash and shares then a capital gain arises unless the cash element is small.

Takeovers

'Paper for paper' exchange

No CGT implications if satisfy conditions

- Clearance
- Acquire > 25%
- Bone fide reason

Mixture of 'paper' and cash

Cash element small
1 ≤ 5% of total value or
2 ≤ £3,000
→ No CGT implications at date of exchange

Cash element not small
1 > 5% of total value and
2 > £3,000
→ CGT implications at date of exchange re- cash received
→ Part disposal

Part disposal of cash element :

Cost of asset sold =

Original cost $\times \dfrac{\text{Cash received}}{\text{Total consideration}}$

- Where consideration includes QCBs:
  - compute gain as if QCB was cash consideration
  - the frozen gain is charged when QCB sold.

Exam focus

Exam kit questions on this area:
Section B questions
- Banger Ltd and Candle Ltd
- Pescara

QCBs and government securities

- Exempt from CGT (i.e. no chargeable gain/no allowable loss).
- If ER is available on the gain at takeover the taxpayer must elect for ER and the gain will be taxed at 10% at takeover.
  - If ER is not claimed at takeover the frozen gain will be taxed at the appropriate rate in force when it crystallises.

Definition

QCB: Normal commercial loan, expressed in sterling and not convertible into shares (e.g. company loan stock/loan notes).

Liquidations

- Shareholders are treated as having sold their shares for proceeds equal to the cash or other assets received from the liquidator.
- A chargeable gain or loss must be computed in the normal way.
- Consider pre-liquidation dividend payment.

Exam focus

Exam kit questions on this area:
Section B questions
- Banger Ltd and Candle Ltd
- Acryl Ltd and Cresco Ltd

Losses on unquoted shares

- Capital losses are normally carried forward and offset against future capital gains.
- Can elect for a capital loss realised on the disposal of unquoted trading company shares to be treated as a trading loss.
- The capital loss can therefore be offset:
  - against income
  - of the tax year in which the loss arose, **and/or**
  - the preceding tax year.
- The shares must have been subscribed for, not purchased.

Capital gains tax – reliefs

In this chapter

- Overview of reliefs.
- Entrepreneurs' relief.
- Investors' relief.
- Principal private residence relief.
- PPR – periods of occupation.
- Rollover relief.
- Reinvestment in depreciating assets.
- Gift relief.
- Incorporation relief.
- EIS reinvestment relief.
- SEIS reinvestment relief.

CGT reliefs are an important aspect of CGT in practice.

Given the examining team's approach to examining real life practical situations they are likely to continue to feature regularly in examination questions.

You may be required not just to calculate the reliefs but to state the conditions, when they apply and the tax implications.

Overview of reliefs

- After computing gains on disposals of individual assets consider the availabilit of reliefs.

- Some reliefs completely exempt a gain from CGT, or reduce the tax payable permanently, others only defer the gain to a later period.

Types of relief	
Permanent reliefs	**Deferral reliefs**
Entrepreneurs' relief	Rollover relief
Investors' relief	Gift relief
PPR relief	Incorporation relief
Letting relief	
SEIS reinvestment relief	EIS reinvestment relief

Entrepreneurs' relief (ER)

- Only available to individuals.
- First £10 million of gains on 'qualifying business disposals' are taxed at 10%, regardless of the taxpayer's income.
- Any gains above the £10 million limit = taxed in full at 10% / 20%.
- Gains qualifying for ER are set against any remaining basic rate band (BRB) before non-qualifying gains.
- The 10% CGT rate is calculated **after** the deduction of:
  - allowable losses, and
  - the AEA.
- Can choose to set losses and AEA against non-qualifying gains first to maximise relief.

  Exception:
  Any losses on assets forming part of the disposal of the business.

- Keep gains which qualify for ER separate from those which do not qualify.
- For 2018/19 disposals, the relief must be claimed by 31 January 2021.
- £10 million = a lifetime limit (partly used up each time a claim is made).

Qualifying business disposals

The disposal of:

- the whole or part of an individual's trading business (i.e. sole trader or partner)
- assets of the individual's or partnership's trading business that has **now ceased**
- shares **provided**:
  - in the individual's 'personal trading company', **and**
  - the individual is an employee of the company (part time or full time).
- assets owned by the individual and used in their 'personal trading company' or trading partnership **provided**:
  - the individual also disposes of all or part of their partnership interest or shares in their personal trading company
  - as part of their withdrawal of involvement in the partnership / company business.

An individual's 'personal trading company' is one where the individual:

- owns at least 5% of the ordinary shares
- which carry at least 5% of the voting rights.

When an individual disposes of goodwill to a close company (e.g. on incorporation) ER is not available in respect of the goodwill, unless the individual:

- is a retiring partner
- holds < 5% of the company's ordinary share capital or voting rights, or
- holds > 5% of the company's ordinary share capital or voting rights, but sells the whole shareholding to another company within 28 days.

Note that:

- "Part of a business"
  = a "substantial part" which is "capable of independent operation".
- Disposal of assets (i.e. not shares):
  Relief = not available on investment assets.
- No restriction to relief if company holds non-trading assets.
- No minimum working hours to satisfy employee condition.
- For approved EMI shares:
  no requirement to hold $\geq$ 5% shareholding.

Key Point

The isolated disposal of an **individual business asset** used for the purposes of a continuing trade does **not** qualify.

Qualifying ownership period

- 12 months prior to the disposal, or
- Where a qualifying business is not disposed of but simply ceases:
  - relief will be available on gains on assets in use in the business at the time it ceased
  - where the assets are disposed of within 3 years of the date of cessation.
- For approved EMI shares:
  - qualifying period runs from the date the option is granted (not when shares acquired).

Applying the relief

(1) Calculate the gains and losses on qualifying and non-qualifying assets separately.

(2) Net off losses relating to the qualifying business disposals against qualifying gains.

(3) Offset all other losses and the AEA against non-qualifying gains.

(4) If necessary deduct any remaining losses or AEA from the qualifying gains.

(5) Tax the gains as follows:

- qualifying net chargeable gains at 10%

- any non-qualifying net chargeable gains as normal at 10% or 20% (remember that qualifying gains utilise the BRB before non-qualifying gains).

Interaction of reliefs

- Other specific reliefs (if available) reduce chargeable gains before ER is considered.

- If also eligible for ER the remaining gain is taxable at 10%.

Exam focus

Exam kit questions on this area:

Section A questions

- Mirtoon
- Farina and Lauda
- Ziti
- Jodie
- Waverley

Section B questions

- Ash
- Acryl Ltd and Cresco Ltd
- Sabrina and Adam
- Max

Investors' relief

ER is only available on a share disposal if:

- the shares are in the individual's personal company they hold 5% of the shares, and
- they are an officer or employee of the company.

On 6 April 2016, investors' relief was introduced. This relief extends the benefits of ER to certain investors who would not meet the conditions for ER.

IR applies to the disposal of:

- unlisted ordinary shares in a trading company (including AIM shares)
- subscribed for (i.e. newly issued shares) on/after 17 March 2016
- which have been held for a minimum period of 3 years starting on 6 April 2016
- by an individual that is not an employee of the company.

IR is subject to a separate lifetime limit of £10 million of qualifying gains.

Note that claims for IR cannot be made before the tax year 2019/20 due to the 3 year minimum holding period. Therefore in the examination you must not apply IR to gains arising before the tax year 2019/20.

Principal private residence relief (PPR)

- Rules apply to house and garden (usually up to half a hectare)
- Owner occupied throughout
  - gain exempt
- Owner partly absent
  - PPR relief available

Relief = Gain × $\frac{\text{Periods of occupation}}{\text{Period of ownership}}$

- If property let
  1 Calculate PPR relief
  2 Then give
     Letting relief:
       Lowest of:
       (i) £40,000
       (ii) PPR relief
       (iii) Gain re letting

PPR – periods of occupation

- Actual occupation.
- Deemed occupation.

Exam focus

You may be presented with an individual's personal circumstances and be required to assess the period of ownership of a property which will qualify for PPR.

You should provide brief explanatory notes for periods of deemed occupation.

Deemed occupation

Conditional	Unconditional
• Up to 3 years – any reason • Any period – employed abroad • Up to 4 years – working elsewhere in the UK (employed or self-employed) – working abroad if self-employed • Must be actual occupation before and after • Condition relaxed if reoccupation prevented by terms of employment	• Last 18 months of ownership

Exam focus

Exam kit questions on this area:

Section A questions

• Mirtoon

Section B questions

• Kesme and Soba
• Noah and Dan

Rollover relief (ROR)

- Relief for the replacement of qualifying business (QBAs).
- The gain arising on the disposal of a QBA can be deferred if proceeds reinvested in replacement QBAs within a qualifying period.
- Available to:
  - companies, individual sole traders, partnerships.

Conditions

- Qualifying business assets
  - land and buildings
  - fixed plant and machinery
  - goodwill
    (unincorporated businesses only).
- Qualifying period
  - from 1 year before
  - to 3 years after the date of disposal.
- Claim is made
  - within 4 years from the later of the end of the tax year of:
    - sale, and
    - replacement.
- For a 2018/19 disposal and replacement
  - by 5 April 2023.

Exam focus

ROR is the only relief available to companies. It is therefore more often tested in a corporate situation.

Effect of relief

Where all proceeds are reinvested:

- The full gain on the old asset is 'rolled over' against the capital gains cost of the new asset.
- No tax is payable when old asset sold.
- Gain deferred until the new asset sold.

Deferred gain is:

- deducted from the base cost of the replacement asset, and
- increases the gain on the subsequent disposal of the replacement asset.

Partial reinvestment of proceeds

Where all proceeds are **not** reinvested:

- The gain that can be rolled over (i.e. deferred) is restricted (i.e. not all of the gain can be deferred).
- A chargeable gain arises
  = **lower** of
  - the proceeds not reinvested
  - the chargeable gain.
- Taxable on the disposal of the original asset.
- The remaining gain is deferred.

Procedure for calculating ROR

1. Calculate the gain on disposal of the trade asset.
2. Determine whether all sales proceeds have been reinvested in qualifying assets.

Proceeds fully reinvested	Proceeds not fully reinvested
No gain now	Gain now = Lower of: (i) total gain (B) (ii) proceeds not reinvested (C)
Gain rolled over <u>A</u>	Gain rolled over (D): D = B – C
CGT base cost of new asset: Cost X Gain rolled over <u>(A)</u> <u>XX</u>	CGT base cost new asset: Cost X Gain rolled over <u>(D)</u> <u>XX</u>

Interaction with entrepreneurs' relief

- ER is only available if the entire business is being sold.

  There is no ER on the disposal of an individual asset.

- If the entire business is sold and all the proceeds are reinvested into new qualifying assets:
  - consider ROR before ER
  - the gains may be deferred
  - ER only considered on subsequent disposal of replacement asset
  - based on conditions being satisfied at that time.

- If partial reinvestment and some gain remains chargeable now:
  - will be taxed at 0%, 10%, or 20% depending on the availability of the AEA, ER and level of taxable income
  - conditions for ER considered now.

Exam kit questions on this area:

Section A questions

- Daube Group
- Hahn Ltd Group
- Harrow Tan Ltd

Section B questions

- Liza

Reinvestment in depreciating assets

Definition

Depreciating asset (DA)

- life of $\leq$ 60 years

Common examples in exam:

- Fixed P&M
- Leasehold property of $\leq$ 60 years.

Method of relief

- Conditions and calculation of amount of relief = same as for ROR.
- Method of deferral = different.
- Gain not deducted from base cost of new asset.
- Gain is 'frozen' (i.e. deferred) and crystallises on the earliest of:
  - sale of DA
  - date DA ceases to be used in trade
  - 10 years from acquisition of DA.
- When deferred gain crystallises:
  - taxed at appropriate rate of CGT at that time (not at the time of deferral).

- Can defer a gain:
  - using a depreciating asset (for up to 10 years), and
  - later acquire a non-depreciating asset, and
  - claim to rollover the deferred gain instead (i.e. defer indefinitely until the replacement non-depreciating asset is sold)
  - provided the deferred gain has not previously become chargeable.

Exam focus

Exam kit questions on this area:

Section B questions

- Bamburg Ltd
- Hyssop Ltd
- Sprint Ltd and Iron Ltd

Gift relief (GR)

The gain arising on a gift is computed by using the market value of the asset.

GR must then be considered.

Recipient
Individual, trustee or company R in UK at time of gift

Applies to
Gifts and Sales at undervalue by individuals and trustees (not companies)

Effect
Deemed consideration = MV
Gain deferred against base cost to donee

Individual donor

Qualifying assets

(1) Assets used in trade of donor or by his personal trading company (i.e. owns ≥ 5% voting rights)
(2) Shares in unquoted trading company
(3) Shares in donor's personal trading company
(4) Any asset where there is an immediate charge to IHT (e.g. gift into trust)
(5) Agricultural property eligible for APR

Asset not wholly used for business

Only gain related to trade use is deferred.
For shares (if own ≥ 5% voting rights) proportion of gain qualifying for relief is:

$$\frac{\text{MV Chargeable business assets}}{\text{MV Chargeable assets}}$$

Key Point

Restriction of (CBA/CA) only applies where donor holds ≥ 5% of shares.

If donor holds < 5% of shares:

- unquoted = no restrictions to GR
- quoted = no GR

Sale at undervaluation

Where the asset is sold, but for less than MV the 'actual consideration' received is ignored

- The gain is still calculated using MV.

If the actual consideration > transferor's cost

- the excess is immediately chargeable
- the remaining gain can be deferred.

The chargeable gain arising now will be:

- taxed on the donor at either 0%, 10%, or 20%
- depending on the availability of the AEA ER/IR or the level of taxable income.

If the actual consideration ≤ donor's cost:

- full gift relief available
- all chargeable gain deferred.

The deferred gain is taxed on the donee later at the appropriate rate when they dispose of the asset.

Emigration of donee

If within 6 yrs of gift the donee emigrates:

- the deferred gain crystallises on the donee
- on the day before emigration.

Effect of relief

Regardless of how the gain is calculated, the deferred gain is:

- deducted from the base cost of the donee, and
- deferred until the subsequent disposal of the asset by the donee.

When the gain crystallises:

- taxed at appropriate rate of CGT at that time (not at the time of deferral).

Election

For a gift in 2018/19, a joint election is required:

- signed by both the donor and donee
- by 5 April 2023.

If gift into a trust:

- only needs to be signed by the settlor.

Exam focus

Exam kit questions on this area:

Section A questions

- Farina and Lauda
- Ziti
- Una
- Snowdon

Section B questions

- Surfe
- Max

Interaction with entrepreneurs' relief

- If ER is applicable:

  - the donor may choose not to claim gift relief in order to crystallise a gain and claim ER now instead.

- This is advantageous if the donee will not qualify for the relief on their subsequent disposal. For example, if they would not satisfy the employment condition and/ or one-year ownership rule.

- If the individual disposes of shares in a personal trading company:

  - gift relief is available:

    - subject to the (CBA / CA) restriction above

    - regardless of whether the individual works for the compan

  - If a gain remains after gift relief (du to the CBA/CA restriction) then ER will also be available provided:

    - the individual works for the company, and

    - it has been the individual's personal trading company

    - for the 12 months prior to the disposal.

Incorporation relief

- Where an individual incorporates his sole trader or partnership business:
  - chargeable gains arise on the MV of the individual assets transferred.
- Incorporation relief is a relief which
  - automatically applies
  - to defer the net chargeable gains arising on incorporation
  - provided certain conditions are met.

Key Point

Where consideration is wholly shares:
- No gain on incorporation.
- Gains deferred until the subsequent disposal of shares.

Where non-share consideration is received:
- a chargeable gain arises on incorporation
- taxed at 0%, 10%, or 20% depending on the availability of the AEA, ER and level of taxable income.

Exam focus

Exam kit questions on this area:

Section A questions

- Farina and Lauda
- Waverley

Section B questions

- Stanley Beech

Conditions	• All of the assets of the business (except cash) must be transferred.
	• The transfer must be of a business as a going concern.
	• The consideration received must be wholly or partly in shares.
Effect	• No gains arise on incorporation.
	• Gains are deferred against the acquisition cost of the shares.
Consideration not wholly in shares	• Gain eligible for deferral: Gain $\times \dfrac{\text{Value of shares issued}}{\text{Total consideration}}$
	• Immediate gain in respect of non-share consideration which is taxed at 10% or 20%: Gain $\times \dfrac{\text{Value of non-shares consideration}}{\text{Total consideration}}$
Future disposal of shares	• On a later sale of the shares, the gain will normally qualify for ER provided conditions satisfied.

Election to disapply	• Can elect for incorporation relief not to apply.
	• Gains on the assets transferred to the company would be taxed at 0%, 10%, or 20% depending on the availability of the AEA, ER and level of taxable income.
	• No gains would be deferred against the cost of the shares, making the gain on their subsequent disposal lower.
	• May be beneficial to elect to disapply if:
	– gains covered by AEA, or
	– shares are to be sold shortly after incorporation (i.e within 12 months) so would not be eligible for ER.
	• Must elect within 2 years from 31 January following the end of the tax year in which the business is transferred.
	• For 2018/19 by 31 January 2022.

Planning points

- Must transfer all assets
    - may wish to retain property with large growth potential to avoid double charge to tax
    - consider gift relief as an alternative to transfer selected assets
    - as goodwill transferred to a related close company is not eligible for ER, it could be efficient to defer the gains under incorporation relief. When the gain becomes chargeable on disposal of the shares, ER can be claimed provided the share disposal qualifies.
- Defers gains pre ER
    - consider electing to disapply incorporation relief if likely to sell shares within 12 months.

EIS reinvestment relief

- Individual:
  - disposes of any asset
  - subscribes for qualifying shares in EIS scheme
  - between 1 year before and 3 years after gain.
- Relief is lowest of:
  - (1) the gain.
  - (2) amount subscribed for EIS shares
  - (3) any smaller amount chosen.
- Individual must be resident in UK when gain realised and on reinvestment.
- Gain deferred until:
  - the disposal of the EIS shares by the investor, spouse / civil partner, or
  - the investor or spouse / civil partner (after a previous NGNL transfer) becomes non-UK resident (e.g. emigrates abroad) within 3 years of the issue of shares.

- Claim within 5 years from 31 January following the end of the tax year in which the disposal occurred.
- For 2018/19 disposals by 31 January 2025.
- Planning point:
  - choose to claim an amount of relief so that remaining gain is equal to the AEA and any available losses
  - work backwards in CGT pro forma to calculate amount of claim required.

If the asset qualifies for ER a claim can be made such that gain is taxed in the year of disposal at 10%.

If a claim is not made the gain deferred will be taxed at the appropriate rate in force when it becomes chargeable.

If a gain deferred was entitled to ER at the point of deferral, it will still be taxed at 10% when it becomes chargeable.

Exam kit questions on this area:

Section A questions

- Pippin

Section B questions

- Capstan

SEIS reinvestment relief

- If an individual:
    - disposes of any chargeable asset, and
    - reinvests in qualifying SEIS shares, which
    - qualify for SEIS income tax (IT) relief

  some of the gain arising = **exempt** CGT.

- Any remaining gain is taxable in the normal way.

- Maximum SEIS exemption

  = 50% of the lower of the

  (i)   gain

  (ii) amount reinvested

  (**Maximum CGT exemption = £50,000** as maximum that can qualify for IT relie = £100,000).

- Relief = flexible, can claim any amount up to the maximum.

- Claim = same as EIS claim:

  For 2018/19 = by 31 January 2025.

- Planning point:
    - as for EIS relief: leave remaining gain equal to AEA and any available losses.

- Withdrawal of relief:
  - If the disposal within three years is:

	Not at arm's length	At arm's length
IT relief withdrawn	All	Lower of: • All • (50% x SP received)
CGT relief withdrawn	All	$= \dfrac{\text{Amount of IT relief withdrawn (above)}}{\text{Original IT relief given}} \times \text{Gain}$

Exam focus

Exam Kit questions on this area:

Section B questions

- Pescara

Key Point

There is no reinvestment relief for VCT investments.

7

Stamp taxes

In this chapter

- Stamp duty and stamp duty land tax.

Stamp taxes may feature as part of a question, however a question will not be set exclusively on stamp taxes.

Stamp duty and stamp duty land tax

- Paid by purchaser.

Stamp Duty (SD) / Stamp Duty Reserve Tax (SDRT)	Stamp Duty Land Tax (SDLT)
Payable on • transfer shares/securities	• transactions in UK property

Rate
• 0.5% of consideration
• SD only:
  – min £5
  – no charge if consideration ≤ £1,000
	• up to 5% of commercial property depending on amount of consideration (note)
	• rates given in tax rates and allowances

Note: Only commerical property will be tested in the examination.

Specific exemptions	
Stamp Duty (SD) / Stamp Duty Reserve Tax (SDRT)	**Stamp Duty Land Tax (SDLT)**

• Exempt securities
  – government stock
  – most company loan stock (unless convertible)
  – unit trusts
  – AIM shares.	

General exemptions	

• Gifts
• Transfers of assets between 75% group companies
  – not available if arrangements in force for purchasing company to leave group
  – SDLT exemption relief withdrawn if transferee company leaves group within 3 years of transfer, still owning the land.	

Exam focus

Exam Kit questions on this area:

Section A questions

- Una
- Helm Ltd Group
- Heyer Ltd Group
- Harrow Tan Ltd

Inheritance tax

In this chapter

- Charge to inheritance tax.
- Lifetime gifts.
- IHT computations.
- Due dates of payment.
- Valuation.
- Exemptions and reliefs.
- Death estate pro forma.
- Payment by instalments.
- Deed of variation.
- Married couples and civil partners.
- IHT and CGT on sales/gifts.
- Skipping a generation.

Exam focus

Inheritance tax regularly features in the ATX exam, often as part of a question involving other taxes too – particularly capital gains tax.

Charge to inheritance tax (IHT)

- Occasions of charge:
  - Lifetime gifts.
  - Death estate.
- Charged on:
  - a chargeable transfer (see later)
  - of chargeable property
  - by a chargeable person.
- Chargeable property:
  - all capital assets / wealth
  - no exempt assets for IHT.
- Chargeable person:
  - individuals.
- Gratuitous intent:
  - transfer must be a gift
  - intention to give asset away
  - not a poor business deal.

Lifetime gifts

- Two types:
  - Potentially Exempt Transfers (PETs)
  - Chargeable Lifetime Transfers (CLTs)

	PETs	CLTs	
Definition	Gift by individual to: • another individual • a disabled trust • certain old trusts (not examinable)	Gift which is not: • Exempt, or • a PET Main examples = gifts to trusts: • (except charitable trusts or those treated as PETs)	
Chargeable	Only if donor dies within 7 years of gift	At date of gift	Additional IHT if donor dies within 7 years of gift
Tax rates	Death rates	Lifetime rates	Death rates
Tax paid by	Donee	Donee, or Donor (gross up gift for tax paid)	Donee

IHT computations

An IHT charge can arise in 3 different situations. The computation in each situation is different and must be studied carefully.

1 Lifetime transfers – IHT on CLTs
2 Death – additional IHT on PETs and CLTs
3 Death estate

In each situation:

- Compute the chargeable transfer.
- Compute the taxable amount.
- Compute the tax.

The chargeable transfer

The first stage of the computation for each situation is always the same; calculate the chargeable transfer:

	£	
Transfer of value:		
Value before	X	– Diminution in value principle
Value after	(X)	– Related property
	——	
	X	
Deduct:		
(1) Reliefs	(X)	– APR – BPR
(2) Exemptions	(X)	– (See later)
	——	
Chargeable transfer	A	

Order of using reliefs and exemptions – see later.

Calculating the taxable amount

Calculating the taxable amount is also the same for each situation. However, the calculation of the available nil rate bands (NRBs) differs.

	£
Chargeable transfer	A
Less:	
Available NRBs	(X)
Taxable amount	X

Nil rate bands

- For lifetime gifts – lifetime tax:
    - Use NRB in tax year of gift.
- For lifetime gifts – death tax:
    - Use NRB in tax year of death.
- For death estate:
    - Use NRB in tax year of death
    - Calculate the available residence nil rate band (RNRB).

- The NRBs will be provided in the tax rates and allowances.

Residence nil rate band (RNRB)

- For lifetime gifts – not available.
- For death estate – available if residential property left to direct descendants (children/grandchildren).
- Deceased must have lived in the property.
- Available RNRB will be lower of:
    - £125,000
    - net value of residential property.

Tapered withdrawal of RNRB

- If net value of estate (before APR, BPR and exemptions) > £2 million
    - reduce RNRB by £1 for every £2 of excess.

Exam kit questions in this area:

Section A questions

- Una
- Brad
- Farina and Lauda
- Ziti
- Kantar
- Pippin
- Florina, Kanzi and Winston

Section B questions

- Surfe
- Pescara
- Eric
- Juanita

Calculating the tax

1 – Lifetime tax on CLT

	£	£
Chargeable transfer (A)		222,000
Less:		
NRB at gift (say)	312,000	
Less: CLTs in 7 years prior to gift (say)	(170,000)	
NRB available		(142,000)
Taxable amount		80,000
IHT payable:		
(i) at 20% if donee pays tax		16,000
(ii) at 25% if donor pays tax		20,000

If donor pays tax:
Add IHT to value of chargeable transfer (A) to calculate gross chargeable amount (B)
i.e. (£222,000 + £20,000) = £242,000

Note that the donor is primarily responsible for the lifetime tax due.

2 – Additional tax on lifetime transfers as a result of donor's death

Perform the following calculation for:

- each gift (CLTs and PETs) in the 7 years prior to death
- in chronological order

Gift 1 – CLT or PET

	£	£
Gross chargeable transfer (A or B)		365,000
Less:		
NRB at death	325,000	
Less: CLTs and chargeable PETs in 7 years prior to gift (1) (say)	(140,000)	
NRB available		(185,000)
Taxable amount		180,000

	£
IHT payable at 40%	72,000
Less: Taper relief (40%)(say)	(28,800)
Chargeable (60%)	43,200
Less: Lifetime tax paid (say)	(10,000)
IHT payable	33,200

Then perform the same calculation for Gift 2 etc.

Notes:

(a) Order of using reliefs and exemptions:

1. Exempt gifts, small, spouse, charity
2. APR
3. BPR
4. Fall in value
5. ME
6. AE current year, then b/fwd
7. Taper relief

(b) Taper relief

Years before death	% reduction
Over 3 but less than 4 years	20%
Over 4 but less than 5 years	40%
Over 5 but less than 6 years	60%
Over 6 but less than 7 years	80%

(c) Lifetime tax deduction:

- cannot create a repayment of IHT.

3 – IHT on death estate

Death estate computation:

	£	£
Value of estate (includes home)		1,025,000
Less:		
RNRB (max)	125,000	
NRB at death	325,000	
Less: CLTs and chargeable PETs in 7 years prior to death (say)	(205,000)	
NRB available		(245,000)
Taxable amount		780,000
IHT payable at 40%		312,000
Less: Quick succession relief		(X)
Double taxation relief		(X)
IHT payable		X

Due dates of payment

1 Lifetime IHT

Gift:	Due date:
6 April – 30 Sept	30 April in next year
1 Oct – 5 April	6 months after end of month of gift

2 Additional IHT on lifetime gifts due to death

Due date – 6 months from end of month of death.

Note: always paid by donee.

3 IHT on death estate

Due date – 6 months from end of month of death.

However, tax is required to be paid with delivery of accounts to HMRC, which may be earlier than due date.

Valuation

An exam question, particularly one involving the death estate, will also require you to value the assets being transferred.

1 Gifts

*   IHT uses the 'diminution in value' principle to calculate the 'transfer of value' (i.e. value by which the donor's estate has been reduced).

	£
Value of estate before transfer	X
Less: Value of estate after transfer	(X)
Transfer of value	X

*   In most cases = value of asset gifted
*   In some cases the diminution in value > value of asset gifted
    *   e.g. gift of unquoted shares.

It is important to appreciate the difference here between CGT and IHT.

For CGT purposes the consideration used for a gift = valued at the market value of the asset gifted.

2 Related property

*   Special rules where same type of property owned by:
    *   Spouse/civil partner, or
    *   Exempt body (e.g. charity) as a result of an exempt transfer to them by the donor or the donor's spouse/civil partner.
*   Applies when valuing a gift or an asset in an individual's estate.

- Value of asset – 2 situations:

   (i) **All assets except unquoted shares**

   $$\frac{\text{Value of individual's share}}{\text{Value of individual's share} + \text{Related party share}} \times \text{Value of combined assets}$$

   (ii) **Unquoted shares**

   Use the same formula, but the 'number' of shares is used in the fraction, not the value.

Exam focus

The related property rules are often relevant in exam questions involving unquoted shares.

3 Other assets

General rule	Open Market Value
Quoted shares and securities	Lower of: 1/4 up rule and the average of the highest and lowest marked bargains.
Unquoted shares	No readily available market price – will vary depending on % holding. Value agreed with HMRC. In examination – value will normally be given.
Unit trusts	Lower bid price
UK freehold property	Jointly owned property: • Valuation ÷ number of joint owners. • Joint tenants – share passes automatically (not via will) to joint tenant. • Tenants in common – share inherited according to will. Value reduced by mortgage – unless endowment mortgage.
Life assurance	On own life = actual proceeds received • For benefit of named beneficiary under a declaration of trust – excluded from estate. • Any other life policy = higher of MV and premiums paid.

Exemptions and reliefs

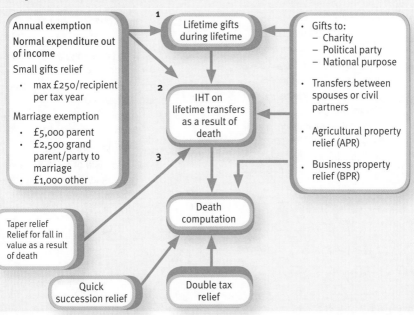

Key exemptions and reliefs

1 Annual exemption

- £3,000 per annum
- Applied to gifts in chronological order
- Used against PET – even if PET never becomes chargeable
- Unused amount can be carried forward one year
- Current year exemption used in priority to brought forward
- Applied after all other reliefs and exemptions have been applied.

2 Fall in value relief

- Applies in the calculation of death tax on PETs and CLTs.
- Donee must:
  - still own the asset at date of donor's death, or
  - have sold it in arm's length transaction.
- Deduct from chargeable amount the fall in value:
  - from: date of gift
  - to: date of death or earlier sale.
- Carry forward original chargeable amount.

Exemptions and reliefs will always feature in an IHT computation – it is important that you can identify when they are available and how they are applied.

Exam kit questions with exemptions and reliefs:

Section A questions

- Una
- Brad
- Farina and Lauda
- Ziti
- Kantar
- Pippin
- Florina, Kanzi and Winston
- Snowdon

Section B questions

- Surfe
- Cuthbert
- Pescara
- Stella and Maris
- Juanita
- Max

3 Business property relief (BPR)

Two key conditions:

- Transfer of relevant business property (RBP).
- Minimum period of ownership.

This relief is extremely important and can be expected to feature in almost every examination.

- Applies to lifetime transfers and on death.
- Applies to relevant business property.

Relevant business property (RBP)

Property	Conditions	Relief
Quoted shares and securities	• Out of a controlling interest • Must be trading company	50%
Unquoted shares and securities	• Including AIM • Must be trading company • Only available on securities if have control based on shares	100%

Assets	• Land and buildings, P&M:
	  – Used by company controlled by donor, or
	  – Used by a partnership in which donor is a partner
		50%

Property	Conditions	Reli
Sole trader	• Unincorporated business or share in partnership • Must be the whole business not individual assets	100

- Available on UK and overseas RBP.
- Not available on excepted assets (e.g. investments).
- Where company owns investments BPR is given on:

$$\text{Value of shares} \times \frac{\text{Company's business property}}{\text{Company's total assets (before liabilities)}}$$

Length of ownership

- Property must have been owned for $\geqslant 2$ years (unless replacement property).

- Where business property was inherited and was eligible for BPR at that time:
  - there is no minimum ownership period for BPR on the second death (successive transfers rule).

- Where business property is transferred from a spouse/civil partner:
  - the combined length of ownership by the couple is considered.

Death tax on lifetime gifts

- Where additional IHT due on gift as a result of donor's death:
  - BPR only available where business property is still owned by the donee at the date of the donor's death.

Tax planning

- No IHT payable on assets which qualify for 100% BPR.

- No IHT saving from making lifetime gifts of assets which qualify for 100% BPR, better to gift on death.

Exam focus

Exam kit questions on this area:

Section A questions

- Brad
- Ziti

Section B questions

- Eric
- Sabrina and Adam

4 Agricultural Property Relief (APR)

- Applies to lifetime transfers and on death.
- Applies to the **agricultural value** of relevant agricultural property.
- Agricultural property
  = farmland, pastures and farm buildings.
- Only available on agricultural property situated in UK or EEA.
- Rate of relief = 100%.

Exam focus

Exam kit questions on this area:

Section A questions

- Una

Section B questions

- Eric
- Sabrina and Adam

Length of ownership

- Property must have been owned for:

Agricultural property farmed by:	Ownership
The owner	Two years
A tenant	Seven years

- Successive transfers and spouse/civil partner transfer rules as per BPR.

Death tax on lifetime gifts

- Retention rules as per BPR.

Tax planning

- No IHT saving from making lifetime gift which qualify for APR, better to gift on death.

Death estate pro forma

	Notes	£	£
Freehold property		x	
Less: Mortgage	(a)	(x)	
		—	
			x
Foreign property		x	
Less: Expenses	(b)	(x)	
		—	
			x
			—
			x
All other assets owned by deceased			x
Debts due to deceased			x
Accrued income			x
			—
			x
Less: Outstanding debts	(c)		(x)
			—
			x
Less: Exempt legacies	(d)		(x)
			—
			x
Settled property	(e)		x
Gift with reservation (GWR)	(f)		x
			—
Chargeable estate			x
			—

IHT payable computation

	£	£
Chargeable estate		x
NRB at death	325,000	
Less: GCT's in previous 7 years	(x)	
	—	
NRB available		(x)
RNRB available		(x)
Taxable estate		x
		—
IHT on taxable estate (40% or 36%)		x
Less: Quick succession relief		(x)
		—
		A

$$\text{Average estate rate (AER)} = \frac{A}{\text{Chargeable estate}} \times 100$$

Less: Double tax relief		(x)
		—
Inheritance tax payable		B
		—

Due date:
Earlier of
- 6 months after the end of the month of death, or
- On delivery of the estate accounts
  (unless paid by instalments – see below)

Allocation of UK IHT payable:

- IHT payable on estate = apportioned at AER (after QSR)
- Tax paid by:

Settled property	Trustees
GWR	Recipient of gift
Remainder	
– overseas asset	Recipient of legacy (tax bearing gift)
– UK asset	Residual legatee (tax free gift)

Key Point

All assets are chargeable (i.e. no exempt assets for IHT at ATX).

Assets that are exempt from CGT (e.g. Motor cars, gilts, ISAs, PPR etc) are not exempt from IHT.

Notes

(a) Repayment and interest-only mortgage and accrued interest. Do not deduct endowment mortgages.

(b) Expenses restricted to maximum 5% of foreign property value.

(c) Outstanding debts payable by the deceased (e.g. outstanding bills and other taxes due: IT, CGT, VAT).

(d) Exempt legacies = legacies to spouse, civil partner, charity, political party.

(e) Gifts with reservation = lifetime gift where donor retains a benefit (e.g. gift of legal title to house but donor still lives in it).

- Bring into estate computation as if gift never made
- can be avoided if donor pays market rate rent to donee.

Exam focus

Exam kit questions with a gift with reservation:

Section A questions

- Mirtoon
- Una

Section B questions

- Pescara

Substantial legacies to charity

- Reduced rate of 36% applies to estates where:
  - total charitable legacies on death $\geq$ 10% x (baseline amount).
- Baseline amount
  = Taxable estate
     plus charitable legacies plus residence nil rate band.
- Can use a deed of variation to increase a charitable legacy to benefit from the 36% rate.

Quick Succession Relief (QSR)

- Look for gifts to the deceased in the five years before death
- Tax credit relief
- QSR = (IHT on first gift) x appropriate %
- IHT on first death = (estate rate on first death) x value of the legacy
- Percentages:

Years between deaths		Appropriate % to use in formula
More Than	Not more than	
0	1	100%
1	2	80%
2	3	60%
3	4	40%
4	5	20%

- Given before DTR

Double Tax Relief (DTR)

- Lower of

  (i) overseas tax suffered

  (ii) AER x (overseas property value brought into estate)

Payment by instalments

- Elect to pay in ten equal annual instalments.

- Only the following assets qualify:
    - land and buildings
    - unincorporated businesses
    - shares or securities where the donor has a controlling interest
    - some unquoted shares and securities (detail not examinable).

- Available on
    - death estate
    - PETs and CLTs which become chargeable on death, and
    - CLTs where the donee pays the tax.

- If asset sold in instalment period outstanding balance must be paid immediately.

Exam focus

Examination questions on IHT will usually involve an element of planning, including advising on how a transfer of assets could be organised more effectively for IHT purposes (see Chapter 12).

Deed of variation

- To change the distribution of assets under will or intestacy.
- Conditions:
    - all beneficiaries must agree
    - must be in writing
    - must contain clause that it is to be effective for IHT purposes
    - made within 2 years of death.
- Situations when useful:
    - to skip a generation where children wealthy in own right
    - to divert family home to direct descendants (children or grandchildren) to use RNRB
    - to increase a charitable donation to benefit from the reduced 36% rate on death estate.

Married couples and civil partners

Exempt transfers

- Inter spouse / civil partner transfers = exempt
    - unlimited in amount
- Exception = if recipient spouse / civil partner is non-UK domiciled
    - maximum exemption = current NRE

Election to be treated as UK domiciled

- Non-UK domiciled spouse / civil partner
  - can elect to be treated as UK domiciled
  - irrevocable election
  - by individual in lifetime, or by executors within 2 years of death of individual.
- Advantage = unlimited inter-spouse / civil partner exemption.
- Disadvantage = subject to IHT on overseas assets.

Transfer of unused nil rate bands

- If the NRB/RNRB has not been utilised at the time of a person's death, the proportion of the unused NRB/RNRB can be transferred to their spouse or civil partner.

- The surviving spouse or civil partner will have the benefit of:
  - their own NRB/RNRB, and
  - any unused percentage of their spouse's or civil partner's NRB/RNRB.
- The unused percentage is applied to the NRB/RNRB at the time of the surviving spouse's or civil partner's death
  - **not** at the date of first death.
- The executors of the surviving spouse or civil partner must claim the transferred NRB/RNRB by the submission of the IHT return by the later of :
  - 2 years of the second death, or
  - 3 months of the executors starting to act.
- As a result, each spouse or civil partner can now leave the whole of their estate to the surviving spouse or civil partner with no adverse IHT consequences.

Exam kit questions on this area:

Section B questions

- Surfe
- Pescara
- Kesme and Soba

Tax planning

Advice for couples:

- Where the couple own assets that qualify for BPR and/or APR these assets should **not** be left to the other spouse or civil partner.

  This is because the legacy would be covered by the inter-spouse exemption and the benefit of BPR and APR is lost.

- BPR and APR assets should be left to non-exempt beneficiaries and other assets left to the spouse or civil partner

  As a result, the benefit of both the relief and inter-spouse exemption will be available to reduce the value of the chargeable estate.

IHT and CGT on sales/gifts

Examination questions dealing with capital transactions may require consideration of both the IHT and CGT implications of transactions.

	CGT	IHT
Sale	Gain/loss in normal way	No IHT – no diminution in estate
Gift during lifetime	As for sale	CLT – tax now
	Gain/loss in normal way	PET – tax if die within 7 years
Gift on death	No CGT	Asset part of death estate
Possible reliefs		
– Business assets	Entrepreneurs' relief	APR/BPR
	Investors' relief	**Note:** On a PET or CLT – reliefs only available if asset still owned by donee at date of donor's death
	Gift relief	
	Rollover relief	
	EIS/SEIS reinvestment relief	
– Non-business	PPR relief	None
	Gift relief if CLT for IHT purposes	
	EIS/SEIS reinvestment relief	

Advantage of lifetime gifts	Disadvantages of lifetime gifts
• Reduces IHT payable on death as assets gifted during lifetime are removed from the chargeable estate. Note: no reduction in the value of the chargeable estate if the assets gifted get BPR or APR at 100%. • IHT on lifetime gifts likely to be less than IHT in death estate because: – IHT = Nil (for a PET) if the donor lives for > 7 years, and 20% (for CLT) – the value is frozen at the date of the gift, therefore by gifting an appreciating asset during lifetime, the IHT is based on a lower amount, and fall in value relief is available if fallen in value – the value subject to IHT is less as lifetime exemptions (such as AE, ME, small gift relief) available – taper relief available if the donor lives for > 3 years.	• Loss of income and use of the capital if assets given away. • CGT may be payable if the assets gifted during lifetime are chargeable assets for CGT, whereas no CGT if gifted on death. • APR or BPR on lifetime gift withdrawn if donee does not retain asset at donor death. Therefore better to secure BPR/APR by retaining asset in donor's estate. • No RNRB available if residential property gifted in lifetime.

Exam kit questions on this area:

Section A questions

- Una
- Florina, Kanzi and Winston

Section B questions

- Cada
- Stella and Maris

Skipping a generation

- Gifting to grandchildren rather then children avoids a further IHT charge when the children die.

- Such planning requires children to be independently wealthy, such that they have no need for the inheritance.

9

Personal tax – overseas aspects

In this chapter

- Tax status.
- Domicile.
- Deemed domicile.
- Residence.
- Splitting tax year.
- Income tax.
- Capital gains tax.
- Inheritance tax.

The overseas aspects of income tax, capital gains tax and inheritance tax can feature as part of a question.

You must be able to deal with situations involving individuals either coming to or leaving the UK and with all of the taxes involved.

Tax status

- How an individual is assessed to income tax and capital gains tax depends on their:
    - Residency status, and,
    - Domicile.

You may be required to assess the residency or domicile position of an individual in a particular scenario. It is essential that you are familiar with these definitions.

Domicile

An individual's permanent home.

Domicile of origin:

- acquired at birth
- normally domicile of father.

Domicile of dependency

- up to the age of 16
- if father changes domicile, individual follows suit.

Domicile of choice

(e.g. where an individual emigrates to another country)

- need to demonstrate severed all ties with UK.

Deemed domicile

An individual can now be deemed UK domiciled for IT and CGT purposes.

Long term residents

- UK resident for 15 of previous 20 tax years, unless not UK resident in any tax year after 5/4/17.

Formerly domiciled residents

- Born in the UK, and
- UK domicile of origin, and
- UK resident in the tax year.

Residence

Definition

An individual will be resident in the tax year if they:

- do not meet one of the **automatic non-UK residence tests**, and

- meet one of the **automatic UK residence tests**, or

- meet one or more of the **sufficient ties tests**.

Key Point

If an individual satisfies an automatic non-UK residence test and automatic UK residence test = non-UK resident.

Resident in UK?

Automatic **non-UK residency tests**	Automatic **UK residency tests**	**Sufficient ties tests**

Automatic non-UK residency tests

Individual in UK in **tax year** less than
- **16 days,** or
- **46 days** and not UK R in any of last 3 years, or
- **91 days** and works FT abroad

Automatic UK residency tests

Individual in UK at least:
- **183 days** in tax year, or
- **30 days** in tax year and only home in UK, or
- **365 days** continuously, some in tax year and work FT

Sufficient ties tests

1 Close family resident in UK
   – Spouse/Civil partner/minor child
2 Accommodation in UK
   – available 91 consecutive days in tax year
3 Substantive work in UK – 40 days
4 Days in UK in last two tax years
   – › 90 days in either year
5 Country tie – Most time spent in UK

Previously resident
= UK R in one of last 3 years
_____

Consider **all five** ties

See tax tables in exam

Not previously resident
= not UK R in any of last 3 years
_____

Consider **first four** ties

Application of sufficient ties tests

Days spent in the UK	Previously resident	Not previously resident
Less than 16 days	Automatically **not** UK resident	Automatically **not** UK resident
16 to 45 days	Resident if: 4 UK ties (or more)	Automatically **not** UK resident
46 to 90 days	Resident if: 3 UK ties (or more)	Resident if: 4 UK ties
91 to 120 days	Resident if: 2 UK ties (or more)	Resident if: 3 UK ties (or more)
121 to 182 days	Resident if: 1 UK tie (or more)	Resident if: 2 UK ties (or more)
183 or more days	Automatically resident	Automatically resident

Note that this table will be provided in the tax rates and allowances.

Splitting tax year

Split year basis (SYB) can apply if individual = UK R in tax year under automatic tests or sufficent ties test.

- SYB = automatic if conditions satisfied
- Cannot disapply SYB

Key Point

- If non-UK R in the tax year
  - SYB cannot apply
  - Will be non-UK R for whole year

SPLITTING TAX YEAR

Leaving the UK

Arriving in the UK

Leaving the UK

Individual must be
- UK resident in current year, and
- UK resident in previous year, and
- not UK resident in the following year

Arriving in the UK

Individual must be
- UK resident in current year, and
- Not UK resident in previous year

Individual leaves the UK and:
1. Begins working full time abroad
2. Accompanies partner working full time abroad
3. Ceases to have any UK home

Overseas part starts:

Date start work abroad

Later of date
– Joins partner
– Partner starts work abroad
Date have no UK home

Individual arrives in the UK and:
1. Acquires a UK home
2. Begins working full time in the UK – For ≥ 365 days
3. Returns following a period when individual (or partner) worked full time overseas

UK part starts:

Date acquires UK home
Date start work in UK

Date individual (or partner) stops working overseas

Income tax

General rule:

- UK resident
  - Taxed on UK and overseas income.
- Non-resident
  - Taxed on UK income only
  - Personal allowance available against UK income for UK/EEA citizens.

Key Point

- All income arising in the UK is always subject to UK income tax irrespective of individual's status.
- A UK resident is always taxed on overseas income
  - the only issue is whether they are taxed on an arising or remittance basis.

SOURCE OF INCOME

UK income

Overseas income

| R and D in UK | NR in UK | R but ND in UK |

UK income

Always taxable whatever the status of the individual
Arising basis

R and D in UK

Taxable

Arising basis

- DTR available
- Personal allowances always available

NR in UK

Not taxable

= Exempt

- No DTR as no double taxation
- Personal allowances available **if** EEA, Isle of Man or Channel Islands citizen

R but ND in UK

Taxable
Arising basis or Remittance basis?
See next diagram

- DTR available
- Personal allowances may be available (see next diagram)

R but ND in UK

UK income

Always taxable whatever the status of the individual
Arising basis

Overseas income

Taxable but depends on amount of unremitted overseas income and gains

<£2,000

≥£2,000

- Remittance basis = automatic
- Personal allowance available

- Arising basis = automatic
- Personal allowances available
But
- Can elect for Remittance basis (decision made each year)
If elect:
- Personal allowances not available
- Possible Remittance basis charge (RBC)

DTR available

If taxed on a remittance basis:
- All overseas income = taxed as non-savings income (including interest and dividends) (i.e. taxed at 20%/40%/45% and SNRB/DNRB not available)

- The remittance basis will still be available to deemed domiciled individuals whose unremitted overseas income and gains are under £2,000.

Exam focus

Exam kit questions on this area:

Section A questions

- Jodie
- Waverley

Section B questions

- Shuttelle
- Piquet and Buraco
- Methley Ltd
- Noah and Dan

Remittance Basis Charge (RBC)

- Only levied if individual:
  - aged ≥ 18 years old
  - is not UK domiciled
  - is UK resident in current tax year
  - has been UK resident for 7 out of last 9 tax years
  - has total unremitted income and gains > £2,000, and
  - elects for the remittance basis to apply.
- Additional tax charge:

	if UK resident for
£30,000 p.a.	7 out of last 9 tax years
£60,000 p.a.	12 out of last 14 tax years

- Added to income tax liability.
- Paid under self-assessment.

Exam focus

Exam kit questions on this area:

Section B questions

- Shuttelle
- Methley Ltd

Double tax relief

Deduct from the individual's income tax liability
Lower of:
- Overseas withholding tax suffered
- UK income tax on that source of overseas income

UK income tax attributable to a source of overseas income
= the reduction in the total income tax liability that would arise if that source of overseas income is excluded from taxable income

To calculate UK income tax on overseas income:
- Always treat overseas income as the 'top slice' of income type
- Calculate total income tax **including** that source of overseas income
- Calculate total income tax **without** that source of overseas income
- Difference = UK income tax on that source income

If more than one source of overseas income:
- Need separate DTR calculation for each source of overseas income
- Take out the source with the **highest rate of overseas tax** first

Exam focus

You may be asked to consider the tax position of:

- an individual coming to work in the UK, or
- a UK individual leaving the UK to work abroad.

Exam kit questions on this area:

Section A questions

- Mirtoon

Key Point

Individual comes to UK to take up employment

- Taxed under normal rules.

- UK residency position depends on intentions when arrive in UK.

- Tax position resulting from residency position:

  - Taxed on all UK source income on an arising basis regardless of residency status

  - Overseas income:

    See earlier diagram.

Capital gains tax

- General rule:

Individual's status	Taxed on
R and domiciled in UK	Worldwide assets
Not R in UK, regardless of domicile	No liability on any assets (unless trading in UK, or UK residential property)
R in UK; but Not UK domiciled	UK gains – Arising basis Non UK gains – Possible remittance basis, see diagram

RESIDENT IN UK?

No — Yes

No branch:
- All gains = EXEMPT from CGT
- Both Overseas and UK gains = exempt
- unless
  - trading in UK
  - temporary absence abroad
  - UK residential property

- DTR available

Yes branch:

UK DOMICILED?

Yes — No

Yes:
- Taxable on Worldwide gains
- AEA available
- Overseas losses allowable

No:
- UK gains – always taxable, arising basis
- Overseas gains – Taxable but depends on amount of unremitted overseas income and gains

< £2,000   ≥ £2,000

< £2,000:
- Remittance basis (RB) = automatic
- AEA available
- Overseas losses available

- DTR available

- Arising basis = automatic
- AEA available
- Overseas losses allowable

BUT

- Can elect for RB (decision made each year)
- One election for both income tax and CGT

If elect:

- No AEA available
- Possible Remittance basis charge (RBC) of £30,000 or £60,000? – see income tax section

---

If RB claimed – are overseas losses available? = depends

- DTR available

Make election

- Binding
- Irrevocable
- Overseas losses allowable – now and forever
- But subject to complicated matching rules (not examinable)

No election

- Overseas losses not allowable – now or ever

Individual coming to the UK

Key Point

Only taxed on gains made after becoming UK resident, subject to domicile rules for overseas assets.

Exam focus

You may be asked to consider the CGT position of an individual coming to the UK and leaving the UK.

Individual leaving the UK

Key Point

- If UK resident for 4 of the previous 7 tax years before leaving the UK.

- UK residents remain liable to CGT even though no longer UK resident **if absent from UK for < 5 years.**

- To avoid the rules and for gains to be exempt: (see diagram).

Exam focus

Exam kit questions on this area:

Section A questions

- Mirtoon
- Brad
- Jodie

Section B questions

- Cate and Ravi
- Max

Temporary absence abroad

Individual leaving the UK for
period of temporary absence

Period whilst abroad:
No CGT

On re-entry into the UK:

Return within five years:
Liable on
- disposals of all assets whilst abroad,
if the asset was owned before leaving
the UK
- disposals after the date of return

Return after five years:
Liable on
- disposals after the date of return
only
- No CGT on disposals whilst abroad
(unless UK residential property)

Non-UK residents and UK residential property disposals

The disposal of UK residential property by a non-UK resident individual:

- is a chargeable disposal, and
- a liability to CGT will arise, but
- only on gains accruing after 5 April 2015
- to the extent that they are not covered by
  - reliefs (e.g. PPR relief, rollover relief or gift relief), or
  - the AEA.

Methods of calculating the gain or loss

Property purchased after 5 April 2015:

- calculate gain (or loss) before reliefs in the normal way.

Property purchased before 5 April 2015:

- rebase the cost to market value at 5 April 2015 (automatic treatment without an election), or

- elect to time apportion gain pre and po[st] 5 April 2015, or
- elect to be assessed on the whole gain[] or loss.

PPR relief for non-UK resident individua[l]

- Only consider period of ownership from[] April 2015 for PPR purposes (as only t[he] gain arising after 5 April 2015 is taxable[)]
- PPR relief available as usual for period[s] of occupation and deemed occupation (see Chapter 6).
- For periods of non-occupation, if the individual/spouse/civil partner:
  - stayed in the property for at least 9[0] nights in the tax year
    = treat **whole tax year** as period of[] **occupation**
  - did not stay in the property for at least 90 nights in the tax year
    = treat the **whole tax year** as a period of **non-occupation.**

Exam kit questions on this area:

Section A questions

- Waverley

Section B questions

- Noah and Dan

Double tax relief

Double tax relief

Deduct from the individual's capital gains tax liability

Lower of:

- Overseas capital gains tax suffered
- UK capital gains tax on the disposal of that overseas asset

Note:

- The AEA amount is allocated against UK gains first.
- When calculating UK tax on overseas gains, treat as 'top slice'.

Inheritance tax

- General rule:

Individual's status	Taxed on
UK domiciled	Worldwide assets
Not UK domiciled	UK assets only

- Deemed domicile
  - An individual who ceases to be UK domiciled remains deemed UK domiciled for IHT purposes for a further 3 years.
  - An individual who has been resident in the UK for ≥ 15 out of the last 20 tax years and for at least 1 of the last 4 tax years, ending with the tax year in question, is deemed UK domiciled.
  - An individual who was born in the UK, who is UK resident in the tax year and was UK resident for at least 1 of the previous 2 tax years is deemed UK domiciled.

Liability to IHT is determined by domicile, n residency.

Location of assets
(only relevant to non-UK domiciled individuals)

Land and buildings	• Physical location
Registered shares and securities	• Place of registration
Chattels	• Location at time of transfer
Debtors	• Where the debtor resides
Bank accounts	• Location of account
Life assurance policies	• Where proceeds are payable
Interest in a business	• Where the business is carried on

Exam focus

You may be asked to consider the IHT position of an individual coming to the UK and leaving the UK.

Individual leaving the UK

Key Point

- Liable to IHT on worldwide assets
  - for 3 years after leaving UK (deemed UK domiciled).
- If acquire a non UK domicile of choice:
  - will only be liable on UK assets once 3 years have elapsed.

Individual coming to the UK

- If acquire a UK domicile of choice:
  - liable on worldwide assets when become UK domiciled.
- If remain non UK domiciled:
  - deemed UK domiciled and liable on worldwide assets when been resident in UK for 15 out of last 20 tax years.

Exam focus

Exam kit questions on this area:

Section A questions

- Waverley

Section B questions

- Ash
- Kesme and Soba
- Noah and Dan

Double tax relief

Deduct:

- from IHT on estate
- after QSR
- Lower of:
  - overseas death duties
  - UK IHT on overseas asset.

Note:

- UK IHT on overseas asset
  = (Amount included in estate)
    x average rate of IHT after QSR.

10

Trusts

In this chapter

- Overview of trusts.
- Types of trust.
- Financial planning benefits of trusts.
- Income tax.
- Capital taxes and trusts.

Overview of trusts

SETTLOR → Property passes into trust → Trustees are given legal title to property

Income is distributed to the income beneficiary ← → Capital is distributed to capital beneficiary

- Trust (also known as a settlement) = Treated as separate taxable person.
- Must have > one trustee.
- Trustees = act in representative capacity in best interests of beneficiaries.
- Trust deed = details trustee's powers and duties.

Exam focus

In recognition of the complexity of trusts, the examining team has confirmed that the knowledge required in relation to trusts is limited to the information summarised in this chapter.

Types of trust

TRUSTS

Definition

Types of trust

Discretionary trust

IIP trust

Definition

An arrangement whereby:
- property is transferred by a settlor
- to the trustees
- to be held for the benefit of one or more of specified beneficiaries
- on specified terms in the trust deed.

Discretionary trust
- no IIP exists
- the beneficiaries have no legal right to benefit from the income or capital of the trust
- any distribution of income or capital out of the trust is at the complete discretion of the trustees

IIP trust
- IIP exists
- life tenant has legal right to benefit from the income of the trust
- trustees must distribute life tenant's full entitlement every tax year

Financial planning benefits of trusts

- A trust separates the beneficial and legal ownership of assets:

  - enables the benefit of owning assets (e.g. income), to be enjoyed by someone (the beneficiary) other than the legal owner (the trustees).

- Can provide an income from the assets for one group of beneficiaries while preserving and protecting the capital for others, for example, setting up an IIP trust:

  - to protect interests of children in situation where spouse remarries

  - to transfer assets under will to IIP trust with spouse (life tenant) entitled to income for life and capital assets passing to children (remaindermen) on spouse's death.

- Can provide a means for an older generation to protect and make financial provision for next generation o grandchildren.

- Can provide a flexible arrangement where different beneficiaries have different needs.

  - For example, a settlor creates a DT whereby trustees have discretion to distribute income/assets to children by reference to individual need.

Income tax

- Trustees = separate taxable person.
- Income tax paid by trustees under self-assessment on income generated by trust and by beneficiaries on income received.

Type	Trustees	Beneficiaries
IIP	Depends on type of income: • dividends 7.5% • savings 20% • non-savings 20%	• Annuitant entitled to fixed amount of income each year (annuity). • Life tenant entitled to the remaining trust income. • Taxed on his entitlement – even if not distributed. • Income maintains nature in beneficiaries' hands (i.e. savings income and other income grossed up by 100/80 with a 20% tax credit, divided income grossed up by 100/92.5 with 7.5% tax credit).
DT	Different rates – calculation not examinable	• Taxed on income actually received in tax year. • Always grossed up at 100/55 with 45% tax credit. • Taxed as non-savings income.

Capital taxes and trusts

Inheritance tax

ASSETS PUT INTO TRUST

During lifetime
– Transfer to RPT = CLT by settlor
– All lifetime gifts into trusts = RPTs

On death
– No special tax consequences
– Assets taxed in settlor's estate in normal way
– After tax assets put into trust

WHILST IN TRUST

RPT
– Principal charge
– Every 10 years
– Max = 6%

ASSETS DISTRIBUTED OUT OF TRUST

RPT
At any time:
= Exit charge when capital distributed
Max = 6%

Capital Gains Tax

ASSETS PUT INTO TRUST

For all trusts
During lifetime
– Chargeable disposal of asset
– Calculate gain using MV as consideration
– Gift relief available on ANY asset as there is an immediate charge to IHT
– Trustees base cost = MV less gift relief

On death
– No CGT consequences on death
– Not a chargeable disposal
– Trusts acquire assets at probate value

WHILST IN TRUST

All trusts
– Chargeable gains on disposals by trustees
– AEA = half individual's AEA (£5,850 in 2018/19)
– Rate of tax = 20% (residential property 28%)
– Trustees pay out of trust fund
– Assessed under self-assessment rules

ASSETS DISTRIBUTED OUT OF TRUST

IPDI ends
– **interest ends on death of life tenant**
= No CGT
= Tax free uplift to MV Remainderman receives assets at MV on life tenant's death

Any trust
– **in any other circumstances**
= Chargeable disposal
– Gift relief on ANY assets as IHT charge

Tax planning opportunities

- Gifting assets into a trust during lifetime
  - means that assets not in settlor's estate on death.
- Assets which appreciate in value can be transferred into the trust
  - will increase in value outside of both the settlor's and the beneficiaries estates.
- Exit charges and principal charges = max 6%
  - may not be significant in the context of the financial planning requirements.
- Trustees of a DT can choose to give income to non-tax paying beneficiaries
  - repayment of income tax paid by the trustees can be claimed.

Exam focus

Exam kit questions on this area:

Section A questions

- Farina and Lauda

Section B questions

- Surfe

11

Ethics, personal financial management and self-assessment

In this chapter

- Professional Code of Ethics.
- Monitoring of serious tax offenders.
- Personal financial management.
- Key investment products.
- Tax efficient investment schemes.
- Sources of finance.
- Self-assessment.

Exam focus

This chapter covers the very important topics of ethics, professional issues, personal financial management and self-assessment.

The examining team has stated that there will always be 5 marks in section A of each examination allocated to the topic of ethics and professional issues.

Questions will require you to provide practical advice based on a particular set of facts.

You need a good knowledge of the professional code of ethics and the investment products available.

You must be able to give suitable advice based on the facts of a particular scenario.

Professional Code of Ethics

Principles

- **O**bjectivity.
- **P**rofessional behaviour.
- **P**rofessional competence.
- **I**ntegrity.
- **C**onfidentiality.

Key Point

Remember: OPPIC.

Exam focus

Exam kit questions on this area:

Section A questions

- Drench, Hail Ltd and Rain Ltd
- Jonny

New clients

Before taking on a new client – a member of ACCA must assess:

- risk to the integrity of the practice on accepting work
- whether firm has adequate skills and competence
- risk of money laundering.

Information to be obtained:

- For a company
  - proof of incorporation, primary business address and registered office
  - structure, directors and shareholders of the company
  - identities of persons instructing the firm on behalf of the company and persons authorised to do so.

- For an individual
  - proof of identity and residential address
  - details of nature and structure of any unincorporated business interests and persons authorised to act on behalf of the business (e.g. partners in a partnership).

On accepting work – a member of ACCA:

- must ask permission from the client to contact old advisers to request information
- if client refuses, should consider not acting for them
- if not, issue a letter of engagement setting out terms and conditions.

Exam focus

Exam kit questions on this area:

Section A questions

- Farina and Lauda
- Snowdon

Conflicts of interest

- Examples:
  - asked to act for another party in a transaction with an existing client
  - acting for both parties in a divorce
  - acting for the employer and their employees
  - where the adviser may benefit from the transaction.

- A member of ACCA may act for both parties if safeguards put in place:
  - the potential conflict should be pointed out to all relevant parties
  - consent should be obtained to act for them
  - the firm must have clear guidelines in relation to confidentiality, and
  - should consider the need to use separate teams for each client.

- Alternatively, consider acting for just one party, or not acting for either party.

Exam focus

Exam kit questions on this area:

Section A questions

- Farina and Lauda
- Florina, Kanzi and Winston

Dealing with HMRC

- Information provided must be accurate and complete.
- Must not assist a client to plan or commit an offence.
- If become aware of a tax irregularity:
  - discuss with client
  - ensure proper disclosure to HMRC.
- Client error:
  - decide whether genuine or deliberate/fraudulent act
  - explain to client the need to notify HMRC
  - prompt/adequate disclosure taken into account when deciding penalties
  - if client refuses:
    - must explain potential consequences in writing
    - if material, consider whether to continue to act for client

- if client still refuses
  - should cease to act and write to HMRC stating that the firm no longer acts for the client but not stating the reason why.

Exam focus

Exam kit questions on this area:

Section A questions

- Ziti
- Kantar
- Gail
- Hahn Ltd Group
- Heyer Ltd Group

Money laundering regulations

Definition

Money laundering = benefiting from or concealing the proceeds of crime

- includes the proceeds of tax evasion.

A member of ACCA must appoint a Money laundering reporting officer (MLRO):

- decides whether to report a transaction to the National Crime Agency (NCA)
- if a report is made, client should not be informed as this is an offence (known as 'tipping off').

Employees

If a member is an employee and becomes aware of irregularities in their firm's dealings with HMRC:

- raise concerns with the apporpriate person
- if appropriate action not taken
  - seek advice from ACCA
- in addition, consider:
  - need to report to MLRO
  - resigning from employment
  - need to disclose under the Public Interest Disclosure Act.

Tax evasion versus tax avoidance

- Tax evasion
  - unlawful
  - e.g. suppressing information or submitting false information
  - client = subject to criminal prosecution / fines / imprisonment
  - adviser = subject to sanctions of criminal law.

- Tax avoidance
  - use of the taxation system to legitimately reduce tax
  - e.g. advice to reduce tax liability
  - also used to describe tax schemes devised to utilise loopholes in the tax legislation.

- Specific schemes have been targeted with anti-avoidance legislation.

- HMRC have also introduced:
  - Disclosure obligations re specific tax avoidance schemes.
  - A general anti-abuse rule (GAAR) to counter artificial and abusive schemes to avoid tax.

    This targets arrangements which cannot be regarded as a reasonable course of action.

- Serial tax avoidance
  - Those who persistently engage in tax avoidance schemes defeated by HMRC = subject to a regime of increasing penalties and may have their details published by HMRC.

Exam focus

Exam kit questions on this area:

Section A questions

- Una

Monitoring of serious tax offenders

Those who:

- incur a penalty for deliberate evasion
- in respect of tax of £5,000 or more

will be required to submit returns:

- for up to the following 5 years
- showing more detailed business accounts information, and
- detailing the nature and value of any balancing adjustments within the accounts.

Dishonest conduct of tax agents

- Incurs a civil penalty of up to £50,000.
- In cases where full disclosure was not made, HMRC may:
  - publish details of the penalised tax agent
  - access the working papers of a dishonest agent with agreement of the Tax tribunal.

Publication of names of tax offenders

- HMRC have the power to publish:
  - the names and details
  - of individuals and companies
  - who are penalised for deliberate defaults leading to a loss of tax of > £25,000.
- Names will not be published of:
  - those who make a full unprompted disclosure, or
  - a full prompted disclosure within the required time.

Giving advice to clients

Considerations of accountants	Factors relating to client to consider
• Know the Professional Code of Ethics.	• Personal objectives.
• Know your client – fact find.	• Current position.
• Best advice – advice must be suitable.	• Dependants.
• Best execution – obtain best price.	• Age.
• Switching – avoid unnecessary transactions.	• Risk acceptable.
• Key features – explain why course of action recommended.	• Tax status.
	• Tax efficiency.
	• Liquidity.

Personal financial management

Individuals must balance the need for income on an on-going basis with investing for capital growth to be used to fund retirement.

Suitable investments will change during an individual's lifetime as lifestyle and income streams change.

Factors to consider when making investments:

- Income available after meeting current obligations.
- Desire to own home and method of financing.
- Need to fund children's education.
- Responsibility to support parents.
- Required lifestyle on retirement.
- Desire to leave an inheritance to children.

- Need to ensure some investments are readily realisable to fund immediate unforeseen demands.
- Likelihood of receiving an inheritance.
- Attitude to risk.

Key investment products

Consider features of different investments to determine if they meet the needs of the client.

	IT free	CGT free	Risk	Liquidity	Income/ capital growth
Bank/ B Soc a/cs NS&I	x	N/A	L	L_1	I
NS&I savings certificates	✓	✓	RF	L_2	I
Premium bonds	✓	✓	RF	L_1	–
Qualifying life assurance policies	✓	✓	L	L_3	C
EIS and SEIS scheme	Tax relief on investment but income taxable	✓	VH	L_3	C
VCT scheme	Tax relief on investment and dividends tax free	✓	H	L_1	C

	IT free	CGT free	Risk	Liquidity	Income/ capital growth
Pension schemes (Tax relief on payments)	3	3	M	L_3	C
QCBs	x	3	M	L_1	C/I
Gilts	x	3	L	L_1	I
Land and buildings	x	x	M	L_3	C/I
REITs and unit trusts	x	x	M	L_1	C
Quoted shares/securities	x	x	M/H	L_1	C
Unquoted shares/securities	x	x	VH	L_3	C/I
Individual savings accounts	3	3	L/M	L_1	C/I

Key

I	Income	H	High risk
C	Capital growth	VH	Very high risk
x	Chargeable	L_1	Immediate access
3	Tax-free	L_2	Access possible but penalty
L	Low risk	L_3	Non liquid
M	Medium risk	RF	Risk-free
		N/A	Not applicable

Tax efficient investment schemes

Special tax relief to encourage investment by individuals in riskier small companies.

	EIS	SEIS	VCT
Qualifying Individual	• Subscribes in cash • New ordinary shares • Qualifying company • Own ≤ 30% of ordinary share capital		• Subscribes • Newly issued shares
	• Not employee or director • Independent of company prior to first issue	• Not current employee (can be director or previous employee)	
Investment by individual	• Max £1 million p.a.	• Max £100,000 p.a.	• Max £200,000 p.a.
Retention period for IT relief	• 3 years • IT relief withdrawn if sold within 3 years		• 5 years • IT relief withdrawn if sold within 5 years
IT relief: Deduct from IT liability	• % of amount subscribed: = 30%	• % of amount subscribed: = 50%	• % of amount subscribed: = 30%

Carryback amount to previous year	• Any amount invested, but cannot get relief on more than £1 million in any one tax year	• Any amount invested, but cannot get relief on more than £100,000 in any one tax year	• No carryback
CGT on disposal	• Gain – Exempt if held > 3 yrs • Loss – Allowable – can convert into IT loss		• No gain or loss whenever sold
Reinvestment relief (chapter 6)	• Gain on any chargeable asset = deferred to subject to conditions • Gain crystallises when EIS shares disposed of or investor/spouse/ civil partner emigrates < 3 years	• Up to a maximum of 50% of gain on any chargeable asset = exempt subject to conditions • Relief withdrawn if SEIS shares sold < 3 years	• No relief
IHT – BPR	• 100% if owned ⩾ 2 yrs		• No BPR
Dividends	• Taxable		• Tax free on investment within annual limit

Exam kit questions on this area:

Section A questions

- Pippin

Section B questions

- Tetra
- Pescara

Sources of finance

Personal

Mortgage

- lowest interest rate (cheap)
- longest term – secured on house.

Secured loan

- cheap, can be long term.

Unsecured loan

- more expensive
- normally < 5 yrs.

Hire purchase

- more expensive
- normally 1 – 5 yrs.

Overdraft

- expensive, short term, repayable on demand.

Credit cards

- most expensive
  (except zero per cent cards).

Business

Equity

- does not need to be repaid
- dividends can vary each year, not tax deductible
- outside influence
- e.g. share issue, EIS and VCT schemes.

Debt

- must be repaid
- interest payments fixed, but tax deductible.

Long term debt

- for purchase of assets, provision of working capital
- e.g. term loan, mortgage, debenture.

Short term debt

- e.g. overdraft, trade credit, debt factoring.

Self-assessment

Filing for 2018/19 returns

- Later of:
  - 31 October 2019 (paper return)
  - 31 January 2020 (electronic return)
  - Three months after issue of the notice to file a return.
- Fixed and tax geared penalties may apply for late filing (see later).

Notification of chargeability

- Must notify HMRC of income or chargeable gains on which tax is due
  - Within 6 months of end of tax year in which the liability arises
  - i.e. by 5 October 2019 for 2018/19.
- Standard penalty may apply for failure to notify of chargeability (see later).

Amendments to the return

- HMRC can amend return < 9 months of the actual filing date.
- Taxpayer can amend < 12 months of the 31 January filing date.

Determination of tax

- Issued by HMRC when a return is not filed by the 31 January filing date.
- Can be issued by HMRC within 3 years from the filing date (i.e. by 31 January 2023 for 2018/19 tax return).
- Assessment = replaced by the actual self-assessment return when it is submitted.

Records

Business records

- A business must keep records of:
  - all receipts and expenses
  - all goods purchased and sold
  - all supporting documents relating to the transactions of the business, such as accounts, books, contracts, vouchers.
- Self-employed taxpayers must retain all their records (not just business records) for five years after the 31 January filing date.
  For 2018/19 = until 31 January 2025.

Other records

- Other taxpayers should keep evidence of income received.
- Must normally be retained for 12 months after the 31 January filing date.
  For 2018/19 = until 31 January 2021.

Penalty

- A fixed penalty of up to £3,000 may be charged for failure to keep or retain adequate records.

Payment dates for 2018/19

Payments on account (POAs)

- 31 January 2019.
- 31 July 2019.

Balancing payment

- 31 January 2020.

POAs = half previous years' tax payable by self-assessment and class 4 NIC (relevant amount)

- No POA if:
  - relevant amount for previous year i ≤ £1,000, or
  - more than 80% of the income tax liability of the previous year was collected at source.

Late payment interest

Charged on:

- all late payments of tax
- at a daily rate
- runs from: due date
- to: date of payment

Repayment interest

HMRC pay interest on overpaid tax

- from: later of
  - date tax due, or
  - date HMRC received tax
- to: date of repayment

Exam focus

Exam kit questions on this area:
Section A questions

- Una
- Kantar
- Ray and Shanira

Section B questions

- Ash

Standard penalties

Applies in two circumstances:

- Submission of incorrect returns
    - All taxes.
- Failure to notify liability to tax
    - Income tax, CGT, Corporation tax, VAT and NIC.
- Penalty = % of potential lost revenue.
- Depends on the behaviour of the taxpayer.

Taxpayer behaviour	Maximum penalty	Minimum penalty – unprompted disclosure	Minimum penalty – prompted disclosure
Deliberate and concealed	100%	30%	50%
Deliberate but not concealed	70%	20%	35%
Careless	30%	0%	15%

- The standard penalty table is available in the tax rates and allowances provided in the examination.

- Penalties may be reduced at HMRC discretion, where the taxpayer informs HMRC
  - larger reductions for unprompted disclosure.

- Minimum penalties apply and vary based on:
  - the taxpayer's behaviour, and
  - whether disclosure is prompted or unprompted.

- An unprompted disclosure
  = where the taxpayer informs HMRC when they have no reason to believe HMRC have or are about to discover the error.

- Taxpayer can appeal against a standard penalty.

Exam focus

Exam kit questions on this area:

Section A questions

- Una

Other penalties relating to individuals

Offence	Penalty
Late filing of self-assessment tax return	
• filed after due date	£100 fixed penalty
Additional penalties:	
• filed 3 months late	Daily penalties of £10 per day (maximum of 90 days) in addition to £100 fixed penalty
• filed 6 months late	5% of tax due (minimum £300) plus above penalties
• more than 12 months after filing date where withholding information was:	The penalties above plus:
– not deliberate	Additional 5% of tax due (minimum £300)
– deliberate but no concealment	70% of tax due (minimum £300)
– deliberate with concealment	100% of tax due (minimum £300)

Offence	Penalty
Late payment of tax • Paid > 1 month late • Paid > 6 months late • Paid > 12 months late	 5% of tax due Additional 5% Additional 5% Applies to balancing payment only (not POAs)
Fraud or negligence on claiming reduced POAs	£ POAs if claim not made X Less: POAs actually paid (X) X
Failure to keep and retain required records	Up to £3,000 per year of assessment

Note that 'tax' for an individual will include income tax, capital gains tax and NIC.

HMRC compliance checks

- HMRC has the right to enquire into the completeness and accuracy of any return.
- Must issue written notice before commencing a compliance check (enquiry)
  - within 12 months of the date the return is actually filed.
- On completion of a compliance check, HMRC must send the taxpayer a completion notice:
  - either stating no amendment required, or
  - amending the taxpayer's self-assessment.
- Taxpayer has 30 days to appeal against HMRC's amendment.

Discovery assessments

- HMRC can raise a discovery assessment if they discover an inaccuracy in the return within

	Time from end of tax year	For 2018/19
Basic time limit	4 years	5 April 2023
Careless error	6 years	5 April 2025
Deliberate error	20 years	5 April 2039

Information and inspection powers

- Covers income tax, capital gains tax, corporation tax, VAT and PAYE.
- HMRC can request information from taxpayers
  - by a written information notice.
- Requests to third parties for information must normally
  - be agreed by the taxpayer, or
  - approved by the first-tier tribunal.
- HMRC also has new powers to
  - enter and inspect a taxpayer's business premises
  - in order to inspect business records and assets.

Appeals to resolve disputes with HMRC

- Taxpayer can appeal against a decision made by HMRC
  - in writing
  - within 30 days of the disputed decision.
- They can proceed in one of two ways:
  - request a review by another HMRC officer, or
  - refer case to an independent Tax Tribunal.

Tax Tribunals

Two tiers (layers) of Tax Tribunal system:

- First-tier Tribunal, and
- Upper Tribunal.

The First-tier Tribunal deals with:

- Default paper cases:
  - simple appeals (e.g. against a fixed penalty)
  - usually no hearing provided both sides agree.

- Basic cases:
  - straightforward appeals
  - minimal exchange of paperwork
  - a short hearing.

- Standard cases:
  - more detailed consideration of issues
  - more formal hearing.

- Complex cases:
  - may be heard by the First Tier
  - however usually heard by Upper Tribunal.

The Upper Tribunal will deal with:

- Complex cases
  - requiring detailed specialist knowledge
  - a formal hearing.

Hearings are held in public and decisions are published.

A decision of the Upper Tribunal:

- may be appealed to the Court of Appeal
- but only on grounds of a point of law.

Personal tax planning

In this chapter

- Personal tax planning – overview.
- Income tax planning.
- Capital gains tax planning.
- Inheritance tax planning.
- Tax efficient income.
- Tax efficient expenditure.
- Tax efficient remuneration.
- Employment versus self-employment.
- Married couples/civil partners tax planning.
- Lifetime giving versus legacies on death.

In the examination you may need to be able to identify and advise on the types of investment and other expenditure that will result in a reduction in income tax liabilities for an individual.

You must also be able to identify the appropriate taxes applicable to a given scenario and advise on suitable tax planning measures to mitigate the personal tax liabilities of an individual.

Personal tax planning – overview

Personal tax planning involves consideration of the:

- income tax
- NIC
- capital gains tax
- inheritance tax, and
- stamp taxes

implications of various courses of action.

Primary aim = usually to maximise the individual's 'net after tax cash flow' position.

Income tax planning

Standard income tax planning measures include:

- investing in tax efficient income
- incurring tax efficient expenditure
- maximising use of allowances and basic rate band
- negotiating tax efficient remuneration
- tax planning for married couples/civil partners.

Capital gains tax planning

Standard capital gains tax planning measures include:

- maximising use of AEA
- paying tax at lowest rate
- effective utilisation of capital losses
- effective use of CGT reliefs
- timing the acquisition and disposal of capital assets
- tax planning for married couples/civil partners.

Inheritance tax planning

Standard inheritance tax planning measures include:

- maximising use of lifetime exemptions (e.g. annual exemption, marriage exemption, small gifts, normal expenditure out of income)

- making lifetime gifts of appreciating assets (but be aware of CGT implications)

- making PETs as soon as possible (exempt if survive seven years)

- effective use of IHT reliefs

- maximising use of the nil rate band

- use of a deed of variation.

Common examination scenarios:

- Recommending tax efficient income and expenditure.

- Considering alternative forms of remuneration
  - Employment versus self-employment.

- Tax planning for married couples/civil partners.

- Lifetime giving versus leaving a legacy in a will.

Exam focus

Exam kit questions on CGT and IHT planning:

Section A questions

- Ray and Shanira

- Florina, Kanzi and Winston

Tax efficient income

- Exempt income – Chapter 1.
- Tax exempt benefits – Chapter 2.

Tax efficient expenditure

	Maximum rate of tax relief
• Pension contributions	45%
• Qualifying loan interest	45% on up to greater of £50,000 or 25% of ATI
• Employment expenses	45%
• EIS investment	30% on investment up to £1 million
• SEIS investment	50% on investment up to £100,000
• VCT investment	30% on investment up to £200,000

Tax efficient remuneration

- Maximising use of exempt benefits
  - Chapter 2.
- Considering the provision of company car versus self purchase and mileage allowance or cash alternative (below).
- Receiving tax advantage versus non-tax advantage share options – Chapter 2.
- Comparing employment packages
  - Chapter 2.

Exam focus

Exam kit questions on this area:

Section A questions

- Florina, Kanzi and Winston

Section B questions

- Jerome and Tricycle Ltd
- Hyssop Ltd
- Methley Ltd

Company car versus self purchase and mileage allowance or cash alternative

Company car	Self purchase and mileage allowance or cash alternative

• Additional income tax liability on:
   – Taxable car benefit
   – Possible fuel benefit.
• No running costs borne by individual employee.
• Employer liable to class 1A NICs.
• Costs of providing car and fuel, including class 1A NICs.
   = allowable deductions against trading profits.
	• If mileage allowance received > AMAP: additional income tax liability and class 1 NICs payable on excess.
	• If mileage allowance received < AMAP: allowable deduction from employment income.
	• Additional income tax and class 1 NICs liability on any cash alternative received.
	• Individual employee bears running costs of car.
	• Employer liable to employer's class 1 NICs on excess mileage allowance and cash alternative.
	• Mileage allowance, or cash alternative, including class 1 NICs
	   = allowable deductions against trading profits.

Employment versus self-employment

- Decision = based on facts.
- No one factor is overriding.
- Consider all of the facts presented and apply the following factors:

Factors to consider	Employed Contract of service	Self-employed Contract for services
Control of work	Employee is directed/instructed in how and when to work by the employer.	Can choose hours, method, location and can sub-contract work to others. Is contracted to produce a result and is not directed in how to achieve that result.
Obligations	Employee has right to expect work and cannot decline the work nor sub-contract the work to others outside the organisation.	Has no right to expect further work once the contract is completed and has no obligation to perform further work.
Risk	No personal financial risk to own capital, not responsible for correction of bad work, paid regardless of whether or not the business is profitable.	Risk financial loss of capital, personally responsible for correction of bad work, risk of no return if loss-making.

Factors to consider	Employed Contract of service	Self-employed Contract for services
Pay	Governed by employment legislation (i.e. regular pay, holiday pay, sick pay) and paid under PAYE system.	No employment rights, paid when work completed and invoice rendered.
Equipment	Employer provides.	Provides own.
Clients	Usually works wholly or mainly for one organisation.	Usually works for many customers.

- Employed = assessed according to employment income rules
  - On a receipts basis.
  - Allowable deductions = wholly, exclusively and necessarily incurred.
  - Class 1 NICs payable.
  - Tax collected under PAYE.
- Self-employed = assessed according to trading income rules
  - On a current year basis.
  - Allowable deductions = wholly and exclusively incurred.
  - Class 2 and 4 NICs payable.
  - Tax collected under self-assessment.
- Advantages of self-employment
  - More allowable expense deductions.
  - Lower total NICs payable.
  - Later payment of income tax and NICs.

Married couples/civil partners tax planning

Income tax

The following income tax planning advice should be given to married couples and couples in a civil partnership:

- Equalise income.
- Maximise use of tax free investments.
- Maximise pension contributions.
- Maximise use of available allowances.

Exam focus

Exam kit questions on this area:

Section B questions

- Monisha and Horner

Equalising income

- Aim = to ensure full use of the couple's PAs, savings NRBs, dividend NRBs and BRBs, and to minimise that amount of tax liable at the higher rate/additional rate.
- Consider ownership of income producing assets (i.e. sole versus joint ownership).
- Make declaration to vary the split of joint income if advantageous.
- Redistribute income producing assets to minimise the couple's liability.

Spouse as partner or employee

- Employment income is not transferable but if one of the couple is a sole trader, consider implications of creating a partnership with the spouse versus employing the spouse.

Partner	Employee
• split income in any proportion, as desired • no tax relief for drawings • class 2 and 4 NICs payable	• income tax relief on gross employment costs • class 1 employee and employer's contributions payable

Capital gains tax

The ability to transfer capital assets between spouses/civil partners with no CGT consequences provides the opportunity to:

- Effectively equalise income (as above) without incurring CGT.
- Ensure both spouses/civil partners use their AEAs each year.
- Ensure gains are realised by the spouse/civil partner who has capital losses.
- Ensure remaining gains are left with the spouse with the lowest income.

Inheritance tax

- skip a generation
  (i.e. gift to grandchildren)
  - no immediate IHT saving
  - IHT saved on death of children
- enter into deed of variation to
  increase legacies to:
  - spouse/civil partner, and/or
  - charity to reduce the rate of tax
- if recipient spouse/civil partner is non-
  UK domiciled
  - consider election to be treated as
    UK domiciled
- leave qualifying residential property
  to direct descendants to qualify for
  residence nil rate band

Exam focus

Exam kit questions on IHT planning:

Section A questions

- Brad
- Florina, Kanzi and Winston

Lifetime giving versus legacies on death

Advantage of lifetime gifts	Disadvantages of lifetime gifts
• Reduces IHT payable on death as assets gifted during lifetime are removed from the chargeable estate. Note – no reduction in the value of the chargeable estate if the assets gifted get BPR or APR at 100%. • IHT on lifetime gifts likely to be less than IHT in death estate because: – IHT = Nil if the donor lives for > 7 years. – the value is frozen at the date of the gift, therefore by gifting an appreciating asset during lifetime, the IHT is based on a lower amount. – the value subject to IHT is less as lifetime exemptions such AE, ME, small gift relief available. – taper relief available if the donor lives for > 3 years.	• Loss of income and use of the capital if assets given away. • CGT may be payable if the assets gifted during lifetime are chargeable assets for CGT whereas no CGT if gifted on death. • APR or BPR on lifetime gift withdrawn if donee does not retain asset at donor death, better to secure BPR/APR by retaining asset in donor's estate. • RNRB not available on lifetime gift of residential property.

13

Business tax

In this chapter

- Starting in business.
- Cash basis for small businesses.
- Flat rate expense deduction.
- Cessation of business.
- Trading losses.
- Partnerships.
- Self-assessment for the self-employed.

Exam focus

For unincorporated businesses (which includes sole traders and partnerships) there is little new technical knowledge at ATX but you must now be able to handle business tax within a multi-tax scenario.

Be prepared to evaluate alternative strategies (e.g. in relation to losses), and to explain your recommendations.

Decision making is also likely to be a key area including 'lease versus buy' decisions and whether it is better from a tax point of view to use employed or self-employed staff in the business.

Exam focus

Exam kit questions on this area:

Section B questions

- Tetra
- Spike
- Juanita
- Meg and Laurie
- Jessica

Starting in business

Key areas to consider for a new business scenario:

1 Income tax

A Badges of trade

= factors used to determine if an activity constitutes:

- trading (s.t. income tax) or:
- an investment (s.t. capital gains tax).

- No single test conclusive.

- Consider (SOFIRM): see table overleaf.

- Additional factors (FAST):
  - Finance method
  - Acquisition method
  - Similar Transactions.

You need to be able to assess a given situation and express an opinion on whether it constitutes trading.

Exam kit questions on this area:

Section A questions

- Una

Section B questions

- Cate and Ravi

Test		Consider
Subject matter	S	• Type of good normally traded vs personal asset. • Income producing.
Ownership period	O	• Sale within short period indicates trading.
Frequency of transactions	F	• Repeated similar transactions indicate trading. • Single transaction may however constitute trading (e.g. toilet rolls case).
Improvements	I	• Work carried out to make asset more marketable may indicate trading.
Reason for sale	R	• Forced sale to raise cash indicates not trading.
Motive	M	• Intention to profit from transaction indicates trading. • Absence of profit motive does not prevent being deemed to be trading.

Remember: SOFIRM

B   Trading income assessment

Exam focus

You are more likely to be given a tax adjusted trading profits figure in the question than have to calculate it at ATX.

However you may have to calculate capital allowances. A reminder of the pro forma is given below

Pro forma: Capital allowances computation

	Main pool	Special rate pool	Short life asset	Private use asset	Allowances
	£	£	£	£	£
TWDV b/f		X	X	X		
Additions not qualifying for AIA or FYA:					
Secondhand low emission cars (up to 50 g/km)		X			
Cars (51 – 110 g/km)		X			
Cars (over 110 g/km)			X		
Car with private use					X	
Additions qualifying for AIA:					
Special rate pool expenditure	X					
Less: AIA (Max £200,000 in total)	(X)					X
Transfer balance to special rate pool			X			
Plant and machinery	X					
Less: AIA (Max £200,000 in total)	(X)					X
Transfer balance to main pool		X				
Disposals (lower of original cost or sale proceeds)		(X)		(X)		
		X	X	X	X	X

	£	Main pool £	Special rate pool £	Short life asset £	Private use asset £	Allowan £
BA / (BC)				X / (X)		X / (X
Small pools WDA						
WDA at 18%		(X)				X
WDA at 8%			(X)			X
WDA at 8%/18% (depending on emissions)					(X) × BU%	X
Additions qualifying for FYAs:						
New low emission cars (up to 50 g/km)	X					
Less: FYA at 100%	(X)					X
		0				
TWDV c/f		X	X		X	
Total allowances						X

The Annual Investment Allowance (AIA)

- Available to all businesses.
- 100% allowance for the first £200,000 of expenditure incurred in each accounting period of 12 months.
- Applied pro rata for periods of account that are not 12 months.
- Available on acquisitions in the order:
  - special rate pool items
  - plant and machinery in main pool
  - short life assets
  - private use assets.
- **Not** available on cars.
- Not available in the accounting period in which trade ceases.
- Expenditure above the maximum qualifies for WDA immediately.
- Taxpayer does not have to claim all / any of the AIA if he does not want to.
- Any unused AIA is lost.

- The AIA must be split between related businesses.

  Businesses owned by the same individual are related where:
  - they are engaged in the same activities, or
  - share the same premises.

  In such circumstances the owner of the businesses can choose how to allocate a single AIA between them.
- Unrelated businesses owned by the same individual will each be entitled to the full AIA.

Writing down allowance (WDA)

- Available to all businesses.
- WDA available on a reducing balance basis.
- 18% on main pool and on SLAs.
- Special rate pool WDA = 8%.
- Applied pro rata for periods of account that are not 12 months.
- WDA adjusted for assets with private use by owner of business.

First year allowances (FYA)

- Available to all businesses.
- 100% FYA available on:
  - new low emission cars ($CO_2 \leq 50$ g/km) (not available on any other cars), a
  - energy saving plant and machinery
- Only available in the period of acquisition.
- Never time apportion for short or long accounting periods.
- Taxpayer does not have to claim all/an of the FYA if he does not want to.
- If any of the FYA is not claimed the balance is put in the main pool:
  - but not entitled to WDA until the following period.

Balancing adjustments

- Assets disposed of:
  - Deduct the sale proceeds from the relevant pool.
  - The amount deducted can never exceed the original cost of the asset.
  - A balancing adjustment may arise.

- A balancing charge (BC)
  - Can occur in any pool at any time.
- A balancing allowance (BA)
  - Can occur in a 'single asset' column at any time.
  - Only occurs on main pool or special rate when the business ceases to trade.

Summary of the capital allowances available for cars

CO_2 emissions
• Low emission:
– Emissions ≤ 50 g/km
– New = FYA 100%
– Secondhand = as for standard emission cars
• Standard emission:
– Emissions 51 – 110 g/km
– Put in main pool
– WDA 18% for a 12 month period
• High emission:
– Emissions > 110 g/km
– Put in special rate pool
– WDA 8% for a 12 month period
• Private use cars
– Separate column
– WDA 18%/8% for 12 month period depending on emissions
– BA or BC will arise on disposal

The special rate pool

- Pools expenditure incurred on:
  - long-life assets (LLA)
  - integral features of a building
  - thermal insulation of a building
  - high emission cars (CO_2 > 110 g/km).
- Pool operates in the same way as the main pool.
- AIA is available on new expenditure in this pool first (except high emission cars).
- WDA = 8% for a 12 month period, reducing balance basis.
- FYA is never available.
- LLA = assets
  - with a working life ≥ 25 years, and
  - expenditure incurred ≥ £100,000 for a 12 month period (but not cars or P&M in a retail shop, showroom, hotel or office).

- Integral features
  = expenditure incurred on:
  - electrical (including lighting) systems
  - cold water systems
  - space or water heating systems
  - external solar shading
  - powered systems of ventilation, air cooling or air purification
  - lifts, escalators and moving walkways.
- Thermal insulation of a building
  = expenditure on thermal insulation on any commercial building (other than residential buildings in a property business).

Exam focus

Exam kit questions on this area:

Section B questions

- Liza

The small pool WDA

- Applies to the main pool and special rate pool only
  - can claim on either or both pools
  - claim is optional.
- Available where the balance on the pool after current period additions and disposals is ≤ £1,000.
- WDA = any amount up to £1,000 for a 12 month period.
- Applied pro rata if period of account is not 12 months.

Short life assets (SLA)

- Each short life asset has its own colum
- Short life means < 9 years useful life.
- AIA available.
- A balancing allowance or charge will arise when the asset is disposed of.
- Beneficial where the asset with a short life is to be disposed of at less than TWDV.
- Not available on motor cars.
- If asset not disposed of within 8 years from the end of the accounting period i which it was acquired
  - the TWDV is transferred back into the main pool.
- Election required for SLA treatment:
  - by first anniversary of 31 January following the end of the tax year in which the trading period, in which t asset was acquired, ends.

Private use assets
(Unincorporated businesses only)

- Separate column for each private use asset.

- Pool is:
  - written down by the AIA/WDA in full, according to the length of the accounting period, or FYA
  - but actual allowance claimed is restricted to business use proportion.

- BC/BA on disposal are also restricted to business use proportion.

- Cannot claim SLA treatment.

- Not applicable for companies.

Exam focus

Exam kit questions with plant and machinery allowances:

Section A questions

- Farina and Lauda
- Ziti
- Bond Ltd
- Pippin

Section B questions

- Liza
- Juanita

Approach to computational questions

For P&M capital allowances, adopt the following step-by-step approach:

(1) Read the information in the question and decide how many columns / pools you will require.

(2) Draft the layout and insert the TWDV b/f (does not apply in a new trade).

(3) Insert additions not eligible for the AIA or FYAs into the appropriate column taking particular care to allocate cars into the correct column according to CO_2 emissions.

(4) Insert additions eligible for the AIA in the first column, then allocate the AIA to the additions.

Remember to time apportion if period of account is not 12 months.

Allocate the AIA to special rate pool additions in priority to additions of P&M in the main or individual asset pools.

(5) Any special rate pool additions in excess of the AIA must be added to the special rate pool column to increase the balance available for 8% WDA.

Any main pool expenditure, in excess of the AIA, should be added to the main pool to increase the balance qualifying for 18% WDA.

(6) Deal with any disposal by deducting the lower of cost or sale proceeds.

(7) Work out any balancing charge / balancing allowance for single asset columns.

Remember to adjust for any private use if an unincorporated business (not relevant for companies).

(8) Consider if the small pools WDA applies to the main pool and / or the special rate pool.

(9) Calculate the WDA on each of the pools at the appropriate rate (18% or 8%).

Remember to:

- time apportion if the period of account is not 12 months

- adjust for any private use if an unincorporated business (not relevant for companies).

(10) Insert any additions of new low emission cars or energy saving P&M eligible for 100% FYA.

Remember the FYA is never time apportioned.

(11) Calculate the TWDV to carry forward to the next accounting period and add the allowances column.

(12) Deduct the total allowances from the tax adjusted trading profits.

Basis of assessment

Exam focus

You must know how adjusted trading profits are assessed to tax depending on whether the business is in its opening, ongoing or closing years.

New business – opening year rules

Year of assessment	Basis of assessment
First tax year (tax year in which trade starts)	Profits from date of commencement to following 5 April (Actual basis)
Second tax year	
(a) Period of account ending in the tax year is:	
(i) a 12 month accounting period	That period of account (CYB)
(ii) less than 12 months long	The first twelve months of trade
(iii) more than 12 months long	Twelve months ending as the accounting date in the second tax year (i.e. the last 12 months of the long period of account)
(b) No period of account ending in the tax year	Actual profits from 6 April to 5 April
Third tax year	Twelve months ending on the accounting date in the tax year (usually CYB, but if a long period of account = the last 12 months of that long period)
Fourth year onwards	Normal CYB

Choice of accounting date

The following table sets out the key points to consider and whether a year end late in the tax year (31 March) or early in the tax year (30 April) is the most advantageous in each case.

Accounting period end	31 March 2018	30 April 2018
Time lag between: earning income and paying tax	Assessed: 2017/18	Assessed: 2018/19
	April year end = profits assessed in following tax year, and tax paid 12 months later	
Time to submit computations	Submit: 31.1.2019 10 months to prepare	Submit: 31.1.2020 21 months to prepare
Overlap profits	None	11 months
Profits **increasing** in opening years, assessments based on:	Later (higher) profits	Earlier (lower) profits
Profits **decreasing** in opening years, assessments based on:	Later (lower) profits	Earlier (higher) profits

Change of accounting date

Conditions for valid change of accounting date:

- Change must be notified to HMRC on or before 31 January following the tax year in which the change is made.
- The first accounts to the new accounting date must not exceed 18 months.
- There must not have been another change of accounting date during the previous five tax years unless for a genuine commercial reason.

Basis periods for change of accounting date:

(1) If the **new date is earlier in the tax year** than the old one, the basis period for the tax year of change will be:

  - the 12 months to the new accounting date
  - this will create additional overlap profits.

(2) If the **new date is later in the tax year** than the old one, the basis period for the tax year of change will be:

  - the period ending with the new accounting date
  - overlap profits from the commencement of trade are off-set in order to reduce the number of months taxed to 12.

As well as knowing the rules you may be required to consider tax planning aspects (e.g. choice of accounting date). Also need to consider the commercial needs of the business.

Exam kit questions on this area:

Section A questions

- Jonny

Section B questions

- Tetra
- Piquet and Buraco
- Meg and Laurie

2 VAT

- Compulsory registration.
- Voluntary registration.

See Chapter 14.

You may be required to determine when a business should register for VAT, identify advantages and disadvantages of registering earlier and penalties for late registration.

3 National Insurance Contributions (NIC)

- A sole trader has NIC liabilities based on his profits together with additional NIC liabilities i he employs staff.

```
            Self-employed
```

Class 2

- Fixed at £2.95 per week.
- Payable on 31 January following the end of the tax year.

Class 4

- Paid on taxable trade profits less losses b/f.
- Rate of 9% of profits which fall between £8,424 and £46,350.
- Rate of 2% on profits which exceed £46,350.
- Paid at the same time as income tax under self-assessment.
- Not payable if over state pension age or under 16 at the **start** of the tax year.

Self-employed individuals who have employees pay:

- class 2 and class 4 NICs in respect of their unincorporated trade, and
- employer's class 1 and class 1A NICs in respect of earnings and benefits provided to employees.

Exam kit questions with NIC aspects:

Section A questions

- Pippin
- Snowdon

Section B questions

- Tetra
- Juanita

Cash basis for small businesses

- Cash basis = calculating profits/losses on the basis of cash received and cash paid in the period of account (instead of normal accruals basis).
- Optional.
- Only available to unincorporated businesses (e.g. sole traders and partnerships) – not companies and LLPs.
- Business must have annual turnover of £150,000 or less.
- Can continue to account on cash basis until annual turnover exceeds £300,000.

Exam focus

It should be assumed that the cash basis does **not** apply **unless** it is specifically mentioned in the question.

Under the cash basis:

- accounts can be prepared to any date in the year
- there is no distinction between capital and revenue expenditure re plant, machinery and equipment for tax purposes;
  - purchases are allowable deductions when paid for and
  - proceeds are treated as taxable cash receipts when an asset is sold.
- the flat rate expense deduction for car expenses (see below) will always be claimed instead of capital allowances in the ATX examination.

Advantages

- Simpler accounting.
- Profit taxed when realised and cash available to pay.

Disadvantages

- Losses can only be carried forward.

Flat rate expense deduction

Any unincorporated business (whether or not they are using the cash basis) can:

- opt to use flat rate expense adjustments
- to replace the calculation of actual costs incurred in respect of those expenses.

Type of expense	Flat rate expense adjustment
Motoring expenses	Allowable deduction = amount using the AMAP rates of 45p and 25p per mile (Note 1)
Private use of part of a commercial building (e.g. guest house)	Adjustment = fixed amount based on the number of occupants (Note 2). Covers: private use of household goods and services, food and utilities

Notes: If required:

1. AMAP rates are given in tax rates and allowances.

2. Fixed amount will be provided within the examination question.
   Private element of the other expenses (e.g. rent and rates) = adjusted for as normal.

Cessation of business

Exam focus

This scenario may be examined in the following circumstances:

- Sole trader sells his business to another sole trader.
- Sole trader sells his business to a company (incorporation of a business).
- Sole trader gifts his business.
- A partner leaves the partnership.
- Sole trader retires or dies.

Exam kit questions on this area:

Section A questions

- Mirtoon
- Farina and Lauda
- Ziti
- Waverley

Section B questions

- Spike
- Juanita

Consider the following taxes for each of the scenarios:

1 **Income tax**

- Capital allowances:
  - Additions and disposals are allocated to relevant pools
  - No AIA/FYA/WDA given in final period
  - Compute balancing allowances (BA) or charges (BC)
  - If business transferred to connected person (i.e. business incorporated)
    - can elect to transfer at TWDV (no BAs or BCs).

- Trading income assessment
  - Closing year rules:
    - Actual profit from the end of the basis period of the previous year until cessation
    - Deduct overlap profits.

2 Capital gains tax

- Chargeable gains arise on disposal of assets (e.g. goodwill, property, investments).
- MV used as proceeds if assets gifted.
- Consider available reliefs:

Sale of business	Entrepreneurs' relief
	EIS/SEIS reinvestment relief
	Incorporation relief if sold to a company
	Rollover relief
Sale to company in exchange for shares	Incorporation relief
Gift of business	Gift relief

3 Inheritance tax

- Consider availability of business property relief on gift of an unincorporated business (Chapter 8).

4 VAT

- Deregister when cease to make taxable supplies.

Situation	VAT position
Individual assets sold	Normal VAT rules apply (Chapter 14)
Assets held at date of cessation of trade	Deemed supply of business assets e.g. P&M, inventory, at MV at date of cessation (Deminimis limit £1,000)
Business transferred as going concern, and • Assets used in same kind of business as transferor, and • Transferee is or immediately becomes registered for VAT.	No VAT – not a taxable supply

Exam focus

Exam kit questions on this area:

Section A questions

- Mirtoon
- Ziti

Section B questions

- Jerome and Tricycle Ltd

Trading losses

Be prepared to apply your knowledge to a particular scenario, compare alternative strategies and explain your recommendations.

Trading losses

- Calculated in the same way as a trading profit.
- Trading income assessment is nil.

Relief against total income

- Available in:
  - tax year of the loss and/or,
  - preceding tax year.

- Offset can not be restricted to preserve PA.
- Offset is restricted if loss exceeds maximum amount (see below).
- Excess loss is automatically carried forward or can be set against chargeable gains.

Relief against chargeable gains

- Available in the same years as a claim against total income:
  - tax year of the loss, and/or
  - preceding tax year.
- Only possible after a claim against total income has been made in the tax year in which a claim against gains is required.
- Do not need to claim against total income in both years first.
- No maximum restriction.

Relief against future trading profits

- Relieved against:
  - the first available
  - trading profits only
  - of the same trade.
- Loss offset cannot be restricted.

- Trading loss is treated as a current year capital loss
- Deducted
  - after the offset of current year capital losses
  - before capital losses brought forward, and
  - before the AEA.

Order of offset

When there is more than one loss to offset:

- deal with the earliest loss first
- losses b/f are offset in priority to CY and PY claims
- watch out for the maximum restriction (if applicable) (see below).

Reduced capital allowances claim

- Loss arising can be reduced by **not** claiming full capital allowances.
- The TWDV c/f for CAs will be correspondingly higher.
- Higher CAs will therefore be claimed in the future rather than creating or increasing a loss now.

Opening years relief

In addition to reliefs available for an ongoing business, special opening year loss relief is available.

- A loss incurred in any of the **first four tax years** of a new business can be set against:
  - total income
  - of the three tax years preceding the year of the loss
  - on a FIFO basis.
- One claim covers all three years.
- Offset cannot be restricted to preserve PA.
- Maximum restriction applies as for ongoing loss relief against total income.

Terminal loss relief

In addition to standard relief against total income and chargeable gains, special terminal loss relief is available.

Relief is given for the loss of the **last 12 months** of trading.

- Relief is:
  - against profits of the same trade
  - of the tax year of cessation, and
  - the three preceding tax years
  - on a LIFO basis.
- Calculation of the terminal loss:
  - (1) loss from 6 April to date of cessation
  - (2) plus proportion of loss in the preceding tax year up to 12 months prior to cessation date
  - (3) plus unrelieved overlap profits.

Business transferred to company

- Business transferred to company.
- In exchange wholly/mainly for shares (80% of consideration).
- Trading losses at date of cessation carried forward indefinitely provided owner retains shares.
- Offset against future income received from company **in any order**:
  - earned income (salary, bonus)
  - interest
  - dividends.

Maximum deduction from total income

Maximum deduction from income other than trading income = **greater of**:

- £50,000, or
- 25% of adjusted total income (ATI).

Therefore restriction will be £50,000 unless ATI exceeds £200,000.

Adjusted total income (ATI):

	£
Total income	X
Less: Gross PPCs	(X)
ATI	X

Key Point

The maximum restriction may be beneficial as it could avoid wasting PAs.

Maximum deduction limit:

- applies to trading losses set against:
    - current year total income
    - earlier years **if** set against income other than profits of the same trade.
- does not apply to losses set against chargeable gains.

Offset against earlier years:

- set against profits from same trade first, then non-trading income
- no restriction to offset against profits from same trade
- restrict offset against non-trading income
- loss that cannot be set off = not lost
    - can claim to offset against chargeable gains, or
    - c/f as usual.

Procedure for dealing with questions involving losses

(1) Determine tax adjusted loss/profits after capital allowances for each period of account.

(2) Determine when loss relief is available (i.e. in which tax years).

   – Different options if in opening/ ongoing/ closing years.

(3) Lay out IT computations for tax years side by side.

   – Leave spaces to insert losses offset.

(4) Set up a loss working for each loss to show how it is utilised.

(5) If more than one loss.

   – Consider in chronological order.

(6) Consider options available depending on whether early year, last year, chargeable gains in tax year.

(7) Offset losses in most beneficial way:

   – Obtaining relief at highest rates of tax.

   – Taking relief as soon as possible.

   – Not wasting personal allowances.

   Watch out for the maximum deduction rules.

Exam focus

Exam kit questions on this area:

Section A questions

- Mirtoon
- Jonny
- Kantar
- Jodie

Section B questions

- Spike
- Jessica

Choice of loss reliefs

* Objectives in choosing the most appropriate loss claim:
  - obtain relief at the highest marginal tax rate
  - obtain relief as early as possible
  - avoid wasting PAs (and the AEA for CGT where appropriate).

* Relief against total income and the opening year relief give earliest relief, rather than carrying the loss forward.

* A large gain in a single year (the year of loss or year immediately preceding):
  - indicates a claim against chargeable gains may be beneficial
  - but must relieve total income of same year first and maximum restriction may apply
  - may result in wastage of PAs
  - maximum restriction does not apply against gains

* relief against gains is at 10% or 20% (18% or 28% for gains on residential properties).

* Relief against total income and the opening year relief are optional reliefs but carry forward relief is mandatory and automatic if no specific claim is made.

* No partial claims allowed (i.e. all or nothing reliefs).

* Losses can be restricted by making reduced capital allowance claims.

* Relief against total income applies to two years but separate claims are required for each year and such claims can be made in either order.

* The best claim may be a compromise of the main objectives (e.g. may accept lower tax saving if relief is given earlier).

Partnerships

Treat like sole traders – each partner is the owner of the business.

Step 1	Determine the tax adjusted accounting profit/loss after capital allowances of the partnership for each accounting period.
Step 2	Allocate these profits or losses between the partners according to the **profit sharing agreement** (PSA) in the **accounting period**.
	If PSA requires a salary or interest on capital allocation:
	• treat as a share in their trading profits.
	The balance of profits or losses:
	• shared in the profit sharing ratio (PSR).
	If a partner joins or leaves during the accounting period:
	• treat as if a change in PSR
	• time apportion profits, apply appropriate PSA to each part.
Step 3	Determine the taxable trading income assessment for the tax year or the loss reliefs available for each partner using their share of the accounting profit/loss.
	Partner joins – opening year rules
	Partner leaves – closing year rules
	Other years – normal CYB basis (i.e. assess the profits of 12 months to a/c date)

Exam kit questions on this area:

Section A questions

- Farina and Lauda

Section B questions

- Tetra
- Amy and Bex

Self-assessment for the self-employed

Tax Year	Due Date for paying the tax	Consequences of paying tax late
Opening year	• Income tax and class 4 NICs = due on the 31 January following the tax year • If 2018/19 = first tax year of trading, due by 31 January 2020 • Filing date = same date	• Late payment interest at 3% for each day payment is late • Additional penalty of at least £100 is levied for late filing of return (see Chapter 11)
Second year and thereafter	• Income tax and class 4 NICs = payable in three instalments • If 2018/19 = second or subsequent year: Payment on account 1: – due 31 January 2019 (i.e. 31 January in tax year of assessment) Payment on account 2: – due 31 July 2019 (i.e. 31 July following tax year of assessment) Balancing payment: – due 31 January 2020 (i.e. 31 January following tax year of assessment)	• Late payment interest at 3% for each day payment is late • Additional penalty of at least £100 is levied for late filing of return • If the balancing payment is late: – as above, plus extra penalties of at least 5% of the amount due will apply (see Chapter 11)

Value added tax

In this chapter

- Introduction.
- Types of supply.
- VAT registration.
- Deregistration.
- VAT returns.
- Output VAT.
- Input VAT.
- Special accounting schemes.
- Land and buildings.
- Partial exemption.
- Capital goods scheme.
- VAT administration.
- VAT penalties.

VAT can be examined in the context of companies or an unincorporated business.

The new topics introduced at ATX are popular topics, but retention of TX knowledge is also essential as all areas can be tested.

Introduction

- VAT is an indirect tax charged on consumer spending.
- VAT is charged on:
  - a taxable supply
  - by a taxable person
  - in the UK
  - in the course or furtherance of a business.
- Output tax: charged on sales.
- Input tax: incurred on purchases an expenses.

Types of supply

Exempt

Taxable

No tax charged

Standard rated

Zero rated

20%

0%

Trader unable to register

Trader able to register for VAT

Unable to reclaim input VAT

Can reclaim input VAT

VAT registration

- A taxable person is someone who is, or is required to be, registered for VAT.

Compulsory registration	Voluntary registration

- Required when:
   – value of taxable supplies (standard or zero rated)
   – exceeds the registration threshold (i.e. £85,000).
	- Traders making taxable supplies (standard rated or zero rated) can register at any time.

Compulsory registration

Historic turnover test	Future test
• Taxable supplies in the last 12 months exceed £85,000. • Perform test at the end of each month. Inform HMRC: • Within 30 days of the end of the month in which the threshold is exceeded. Registered from: • The first day of the second month after taxable supplies exceeded the threshold. • An agreed earlier date.	• Taxable supplies in the next 30 days is expected to exceed £85,000. • Perform test constantly. • By the end of the 30 day period in which the threshold is expected to be exceeded. • From the start of the 30 day period.
If taxable supplies are wholly zero rated there is an exemption from compulsory registration.	

Exam focus

Exam kit questions on this area:

Section A questions

- Kantar
- Sprint Ltd and Iron Ltd
- Ray and Shanira
- Heyer Ltd Group

Section B questions

- Ash

Voluntary registration

Advantages	Disadvantages
• Input tax recoverable.	• Output charged on sales:
• If making zero rated supplies:	– if make standard rated supplies to customers who are not VAT registere will be an additional cost to them
– VAT returns will show VAT repayable	– may affect competitiveness.
– can register for monthly returns to aid cashflow.	• VAT administration burden.
• Avoids penalties for late registration.	
• May give the impression of a more substantial business.	

Exam focus

Exam kit questions on this area:

Section B questions

• Ash

Deregistration

Compulsory deregistration	Voluntary deregistration
• When cease to make taxable supplies. Inform HMRC: • within 30 days of ceasing to make taxable supplies. Deregistered from: • date of cessation, or • an agreed earlier date.	• If value of expected taxable supplies in the next 12 months will not be > £83,000. • At any time when above test satisfied. • Date of request for deregistration, or • An agreed later date.

- Consequences of deregistration
  - Deemed to make a supply of business assets held at date when cease to be a taxable person (e.g. capital items, trading inventory).
  - Exclude items if no input tax reclaimed on them (e.g. cars purchased with private use).
  - No output charge if VAT on deemed supply is ≤ £1,000.

Exam focus

Exam kit questions on this area:

Section A questions

- Mirtoon
- Jodie

Section B questions

- Jerome and Tricycle Ltd
- Acryl Ltd and Cresco Ltd

VAT returns

- Normally quarterly.
- If receive VAT repayments can elect for monthly returns.
- VAT payable
  = (Total output tax less total input tax).
- A businesses must:
  - file the return online, and
  - pay electronically,
  - within one month and seven days of the end of the VAT period.
- VAT inclusive amounts:
  - VAT
    = Gross amount x 20/120 (or 1/6)
  - Net amount
    = Gross amount x 100/120 (or 5/6)

Output VAT

Value of supply

- Consideration in money:
  - Trader's VAT exclusive selling price less the amount of any trade or bulk buy discounts offered.
- If a prompt payment discount is offered, VAT is charged on the amount received.
- Consideration not in money or money and something other than money:
  - Open market value.
- Gifts of inventory and non-current assets
  - Replacement value.
- Certain gifts are not taxable supplies:
  - goods which cost ≤ £50 per customer, per year, and
  - any number of business samples, and
  - gifts of service (to employees or customers).

- Goods for own use
  - Replacement value if purchased for business purposes (no output VAT if purchased for private purposes).

Relief for irrecoverable debts

- Relief available where:
  - output VAT in respect of an outstanding debt has been accounted for and paid by the supplier
  - the supplier has written the debt off in the accounts as irrecoverable
  - six months has elapsed since the debt was due for payment.
- Claim the relief as input VAT on the VAT return.
- Customers who have not paid for goods/ services within 6 months of the due date must repay the input tax they have previously claimed.

Transfer of a going concern (TOGC)

- Transfer of a business is not treated as a supply for VAT purposes, therefore:
    - no output VAT charged on assets transferred by seller
    - no input VAT recoverable by purchaser.
- Conditions (all must be satisfied):
    - business transferred as a going concern
    - no significant break in trading
    - to a taxable person (VAT registered or liable to become VAT registered)
    - same type of trade carried on after the transfer.
- A building on which an option to tax has been made cannot be part of the TOGC
    - unless the purchaser also opts to tax the building.

- Transferee may:
    - take over VAT registration of the transferor, but
    - also inherits the transferor's VAT liabilities.
- Where there is a transfer of a business which does not meet the VAT TOGC conditions:
    - VAT is payable on the individual assets transferred.

Exam focus

Exam kit questions on this area:

Section A questions

- Ziti

Section B questions

- Jerome and Tricycle Ltd

Input VAT

- Conditions to reclaim input VAT:

  - Must be taxable person when incurred
    (exception = pre-registration VAT).

  - Supply must have been to the person making the claim.

  - Supply must be properly supported, normally by VAT invoice.

  - Goods/services must be used for business purposes.

- No distinction between capital and revenue expenditure.

  - Input VAT is recoverable on the purchase of capital assets as well as revenue expenditure.

Non-deductible VAT

- Business entertainment

  - includes hospitality of any kind (e.g. food, drink, accommodation)

  - excludes staff entertainment, and entertaining overseas customers.

- Motor cars

  - Purchase – only recoverable if used 100% for business.

  - Leasing – if partly used for private purposes, only 50% of VAT on leasing charge recoverable.

  - Motor expenses – provided some business use, 100% recoverable.

  - If input VAT is not recovered on purchase, output VAT is not charged on the disposal.

- Fuel – Input tax 100% deductible even if private fuel provided

  Output VAT chargeable on:

  - fuel reimbursed in full
    - amount reimbursed.
  - not reimbursed in full
    - fuel scale charge (based on CO_2 emissions)
    - scale charge will be provided in examination.

- Private use
  - input VAT cannot be claimed on goods or services not used for business purposes
  - an apportionment is made for partial private use.

- Goods for own use
  - input VAT recoverable if purchased for business purposes (not recoverable if purchased for private purposes).

Key Point

Where VAT is not recoverable on capital expenditure (e.g. purchase of a car) capital allowances are claimed on the VAT inclusive cost.

Pre-registration input VAT

Conditions to reclaim input VAT:

Goods	Services
• Acquired in the 4 years before registration, and • Still held at date of registration	• Supplied in the 6 months before registration

Special accounting schemes

- Three special schemes aimed at small businesses.

Cash accounting scheme

Operation	Conditions	Advantages
• VAT accounted for on cash payments and cash receipts	• Taxable turnover ≤ £1,350,000 • VAT payments and returns must be up to date • Must leave the scheme if taxable turnover > £1,600,000	• Do not pay output tax until receive payment from customer • Provides automatic relief for irrecoverable debts

Exam kit questions on this area:

Section A questions

- Drench, Hail Ltd and Rain Ltd

Flat rate scheme

Operation	Conditions	Advantages
• Flat rate of VAT applied to total turnover (including exempt supplies and VAT) • Flat rate determined by trade sector • Flat rate only used to simplify preparation of VAT return – still need to issue tax invoices	• Taxable supplies for the next 12 months ≤ £150,000 • Businesses are eligible to stay in the scheme until their VAT inclusive turnover exceeds £230,000	• Reduces administration – do not need to account for VAT on individual purchases • May reduce total VAT payable

Exam focus

Exam kit questions on this area:

Section B questions

• Bamburg Ltd

Annual accounting scheme

Operation	Conditions	Advantages

• One VAT return prepared a year
• Return due:
  2 months after end of annual VAT period
• Payments on account (POA):
  – 9 POA due in months 4 – 12
  – each POA is 10% of VAT for previous year
• Balancing payment due with the VAT return on same date
• New businesses base POA on estimated VAT liability
	• Taxable turnover $\leqslant$ £1,350,000
	• VAT payments and returns must be up to date
	• Must leave scheme if taxable turnover > £1,600,000
		• Reduces administration
		• Regular payments can help cashflow

Exam focus

Exam kit questions on this area:

Section B questions

• Harrow Tan Ltd

Land and buildings

Types of supply

Supplies of land and buildings in the UK can be either be zero rated, standard rated or exempt.

Opting to tax

A VAT registered vendor or lessor of a building can opt to waive the exemption of the building. This is usually referred to as 'opting to tax.'

Exam focus

Exam kit questions on this area:

Section A questions

- Janus plc Group
- Flame plc Group
- Ziti
- Maria and Granada Ltd

Section B questions

- Achiote Ltd

OPTION TO TAX

CONDITIONS

- Election must be filed within 30 days of signing.
- Can be withdrawn within initial six month cooling off period or after 20 years otherwise irrevocable.
- Election cannot be made for a part of a building, although the election can be made separately for each property owned.

IMPACT

- Supply becomes a taxable supply.
- Input tax in respect of the building can be recovered.
- Future supplies of the building (e.g. sales or rents, must be standard-rated).
- New owners are not bound by a previous owner's election, except for transfers within a VAT group (Chapter 16).

Partial exemption

Traders who make both taxable and exempt supplies:

− only part of the input tax is recoverable.

Exam focus

Exam kit questions on this area:

Section A questions

- Janus plc Group
- Snowdon

Section B questions

- Spetz Ltd Group
- Nocturne Ltd

Methods of determining recoverable input tax

The standard method for determining the amount of recoverable input VAT is as follows

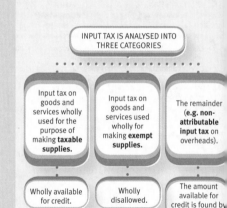

- Non-attributable input VAT reclaimable:

$$\frac{\text{Total taxable supplies (exc. VAT)}}{\text{Total supplies}} = \%$$

- Exclude supplies of capital goods
- Round % up to next whole number
- Any other reasonable method of apportionment can be agreed with HMRC

- Can either calculate the reclaimable % each quarter or can use last year's %

Annual adjustment

- Recalculate recoverable % at the end of each accounting period based on actual supplies for the year.

- Any under or over-claim accounted for in first VAT return of next year, or can bring forward to final VAT return for this period.

De minimis limits

- All input tax (including that relating wholly or partly to exempt supplies) may be recovered if the business is below the de minimis limits.

- Three tests to see whether a business is de minimis:

  (1) **Total input tax ≤ £625 per month** on average, and
  Value of **exempt supplies ≤ 50%** of value of **total supplies**

  (2) **Total input tax less input tax directly attributable to taxable supplies≤ £625 per month** on average, and
  Value of **exempt supplies ≤ 50%** of value of **total supplies**

  (3) **Input tax relating to exempt supplies ≤ £625 per month** on average, and
  Input tax relating to exempt supplies ≤ 50% of total input VAT

- Only need to satisfy one test.
- If business was de minimis last year:
  - can provisionally recover all VAT this year (unless input tax expected to be > £1million).
- Status must be reviewed at end of the accounting period based on whole year.
- Annual adjustment made as above, if necessary.

Annual test

- The business can apply the de minimis tests once a year rather than every return period if:
  - the business was de minimis in the previous year, and
  - the annual test is applied consistently throughout the current year, and
  - the input VAT for the current year is not expected to exceed £1 million.

- This means that the business can provisionally recover all input VAT relating to exempt supplies in each return period without having to perform de minimis calculations.
- At the end of the accounting period, the de minimis status must be reviewed based on the year as a whole and an annual adjustment made if necessary.

Capital goods scheme

- Applies to partially exempt traders who spend large sums on land and buildings or computer equipment.
- Initial deduction of input tax is made in the ordinary way and then reviewed over a set adjustment period.

- Assets covered by the scheme:

Item	Value	Adjustment period
Land and buildings	£250,000 or more	10 years (5 years where subject to a lease of less than 10 years at acquisition)
Computers and computer equipment	£50,000 or more	5 years

A trader making say 70% taxable supplies and 30% exempt supplies:

- can initially reclaim 70% of the input VAT charged in respect of a building

- adjustments are made over the next 10 (or 5) years if the proportion of exempt supplies changes.

The annual adjustment is:

$$\frac{\text{Total input tax}}{10 \text{ or } 5 \text{ years}} \times (\% \text{ now} - \% \text{ in the original year})$$

Disposal of building in adjustment period

- normal annual adjustment
- further adjustment

if disposal:	for remainder of adjustment period assume
taxable	100% taxable use
exempt	0% taxable use

Exam focus

Exam kit questions on this area:

Section A questions

- Janus plc Group
- Bond Ltd

Section B questions

- Hyssop Ltd

VAT administration

VAT records

- Must keep records of all goods/services received and supplied, sufficient to allow the return to be completed and allow HMRC to check the return.

- Retain records for 6 years.

- Type of records to retain:

    - copies of VAT invoices issued

    - record of outputs (e.g. sales day book)

    - evidence to support recovery of input tax

    - VAT account.

VAT penalties

- **Standard penalties** apply in the same way for income tax, CGT, corporation tax and VAT.

- Depends on the behaviour of the taxpayer (see Chapter 11).

- Errors in VAT returns can give rise to

    - Default interest, and

    - Standard penalty for the submission of an incorrect VAT return.

Specific penalty relating to VAT

- The default surcharge.

Default surcharge

Arises	• Return submitted late, or
	• VAT paid late
First default	• HMRC serve a surcharge liability notice
	• Specifies a surcharge period:
	– ending 12 months after the end of the VAT period to which the default relates
Further defaults	• Surcharge period extended to 12 months after the end of the VAT period in which the latest default relates
	• If default involves late payment of VAT – Surcharge penalty levied

Surcharges	Default in surcharge period	% of VAT unpaid
	First	2%
	Second	5%
	Third	10%
	Fourth and more	15%

Note:

• Surcharge assessments at rates below 10% will not be issued for amounts of < £400.

• Where rate is 10% or more, the minimum surcharge is £30.

Error on VAT returns

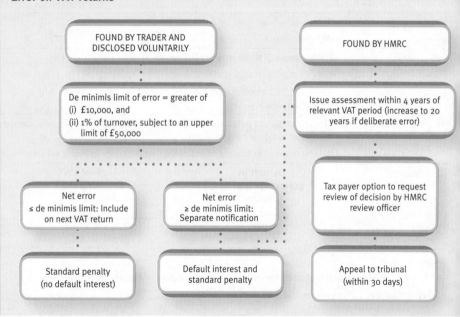

FOUND BY TRADER AND DISCLOSED VOLUNTARILY

FOUND BY HMRC

De minimis limit of error = greater of
(i) £10,000, and
(ii) 1% of turnover, subject to an upper limit of £50,000

Issue assessment within 4 years of relevant VAT period (increase to 20 years if deliberate error)

Net error ≤ de minimis limit: Include on next VAT return

Net error ≥ de minimis limit: Separate notification

Tax payer option to request review of decision by HMRC review officer

Standard penalty (no default interest)

Default interest and standard penalty

Appeal to tribunal (within 30 days)

Default interest

Arises	• HMRC raise an assessment to collect undeclared/overclaimed VAT.
	• Voluntary disclosure of errors exceeding de minimis limit.
Charged	• From due date of payment to actual date of payment.

15

Corporation tax – liability and losses

In this chapter

- Chargeable accounting periods.
- Taxable total profits computation.
- Corporation tax payable.
- Trading profits – specific issues for companies.
- Capital allowances.
- Long period of account.
- Self-assessment.
- Penalties.
- Trading losses – single company.
- Restriction of carry forward of losses.
- Non-trading losses.

Corporation tax is very important.

Questions on corporation tax will regularly feature in the examination and you need to be able to prepare a corporation tax computation, as well as explain the tax implications of company transactions.

This chapter revises the key issues in preparing a corporation tax computation, summarises the self-assessment rules and sets out the options for a single company making losses.

Chargeable accounting periods (CAPs)

- Corporation tax computation required for each CAP.
- Cannot be longer than 12 months.
- Starts:
  - when start to trade
  - previous CAP ends.
- Ends:
  - 12 months after start
  - end of period of account (i.e. company's period for which it draws up accounts)
  - cease to trade/be resident in UK
  - go into administration/liquidation.

Taxable total profits computation

ABC Ltd
Corporation tax computation for year ended 31 March 2019

	Notes	£
Trading profits	(a)	X
Interest income	(b)	X
Overseas income	(c)	X
Property income		X
Net chargeable gains	(d)	X
Total profits		X
Less: QCD relief	(e)	(X)
Taxable total profits (TTP)	(f)	X

Corporation tax payable

	Notes	
• Tax liability:		

		£
TTP × 19%	(g)	X
Less: DTR		(X)
CT payable		X

Notes

(a) Trading profit = Adjusted trading profit less capital allowances. Adjustments include interest and royalties paid for trade purposes.

(b) Interest income includes on non-trading loan relationships (i.e. interest receivable and payable).

(c) Overseas income may include rental income, interest income and branch profits, but excludes overseas dividends.

(d) Net chargeable gains = capital gains less all capital losses:

- Indexation allowance (IA) available up to December 2017, or date of disposal if earlier

- Indexation factors given in examination

- cannot create or increase a capital loss

- no AEA

- consider rollover relief and substantial shareholding exemption

(e) Qualifying charitable donations (QCDs)

- includes all charitable donations by company which are not allowed as a trading expense.

(f) Dividend income from UK and overseas companies is never chargeable to corporation tax and not included in TTP.

However, is included in augmented profits for instalment purposes.

(g) The rate of corporation tax is fixed for each financial year. The rate for FY2018 and FY2017 is 19%. The rate for FY2016 was 20%.

For CAPs straddling 31 March 2017 a two part computation is required.

Trading profits – specific issues for companies

- Loan relationships
- Goodwill and other intangibles
- Research and development
- Gains on shares of companies

Loan relationships

All income, expenses, capital and revenue arising from loans is taxed under the loan relationship rules.

	Trading loan	Non-trading loan
Example	Loan notes issued to raise funds to acquire P&M	Loan to acquire investment property or a subsidiary
Income/ capital profit	Trading income	Interest income
Expense/ capital loss	Deduct from trading income	Deduct from interest income Relief available for net loss

Exam focus

Exam kit questions on this area:

Section A questions

- Helm Ltd Group

Section B questions

- Banger Ltd and Candle Ltd

Goodwill and other intangibles

Intangibles (excluding goodwill)

- Intangible assets acquired by companies are not capital assets for capital gains purposes, but follow accounting treatment.

- Debits and credits, income and capital = part of trading income assessment.

- A company can claim a 4% WDA p.a. if no amortisation in financial accounts or amortisation rate is < 4% p.a.

- On sale of intangibles:

    - profit or loss is assessable/deductible for trading purposes.

- Accounting profit or loss will give rise to an identical tax profit or loss:

    - unless the 4% election is made

    - in which case a tax adjustment must be made by comparing the accounting profit to the taxable profit.

Goodwill

- The treatment of goodwill differs from other intangible assets.

- Amortisation or impairments of goodwill are disallowable for corporation tax.

- Profit/loss on disposal = proceeds less cost (as book value for tax = cost)

    - Profit on disposal = taxable as part of trading profits

    - Loss on disposal = relieved as a non-trading debit.

Special intangibles rollover relief

- If a new intangible is acquired:

    - within 12 months before or up to 36 months after

    - part of the taxable credit may be deferred.

- Applies to goodwill and other intangible

- Maximum deferral is:

	£
Lower of:	
– Proceeds	
– Amount reinvested	X
Less: Cost of original intangible	(X)
	X

Exam focus

Exam kit questions on this area:

Section A questions

- Janus plc Group

Section B questions

- Cinnabar Ltd
- Maria and Granada Ltd
- Achiote Ltd

Research and development expenditure (R&D)

- Expenditure on R&D as defined by GAAP qualifies for certain reliefs for companies.

- Expenditure includes:

    - Staffing costs
    - Agency staff
    - Materials, water, fuel and power
    - Software
    - Subcontractor payments

Exam focus

Exam kit questions on this area:

Section B questions

- Sank Ltd and Kurt Ltd
- Cinnabar Ltd
- Damiana plc

- Relief as follows:

Small and medium sized company
+ 130% allowable
Repayment = 14.5% x lower of: • trading loss • 230% of qualifying R&D expenditure

Optional 'above the line tax credit' for large companies

Large companies can:

- Opt to claim a tax credit against their corporation tax liability = 12% of the qualifying R&D expenditure
- Method of relief:
  - deducted from the CT liability, and
  - include as taxable income in TTP (taxed at 19%).

- Net benefit of 9.72%
- If no CT liability or insufficient liability to net off all the tax credit the excess will b
  - paid in cash, net of tax
  - up to max = PAYE/NIC liability for R&D employees for CAP
  - if repayable tax credit > max cash repayment allowed:

    the remaining tax credit can be:
  - carried forward and set against the first available future CT liability, or
  - group relieved.

Gains on shares for companies

Substantial shareholding exemption

- Disposal of shares out of a substantial shareholding (SSE)
  = exempt from corporation tax.

- Substantial shareholding
  = where company has owned:

  - ≥ 10% interest in the shares

  - for ≥ 12 months continuously

  - in the last 6 years.

- If shares held < 12 months exemption still applies if:

  - shares disposed of are in a new company, and

  - trade and assets of another 75% group company are transferred to that new company prior to sale of shares, and

  - trade and assets have been owned by group for ≥ 12 months in last 6 years.

Exam focus

Exam kit questions on this area:

Section A questions

- Janus plc Group

- Harrow Tan Ltd

- Helm Ltd Group

- Sprint Ltd and Iron Ltd

- Gail

Section B questions

- Cinnabar Ltd

- Acryl Ltd and Cresco Ltd

- Achiote Ltd

If SSE does not apply

Gains on shares for companies

- If disposal not out of a substantial shareholding:
  - use matching rules for companies, and
  - calculate a gain.
- The matching rules for company disposal of shares is:
  - Same day acquisitions
  - Acquisitions in the previous nine days (FIFO basis)
  - Acquisitions from the share pool.
- Calculation of gains
  - No IA given on same day acquisitions and purchases in previous 9 days
  - IA is available on share pool shares.

The share pool

The share pool for companies is different t
the share pool for individuals as follows:

- It contains shares in the same compan
  of the same class, purchased up to 9
  days before the date of disposal.
- The pool keeps a record of the:
  - number of shares acquired and so
  - cost of the shares, and
  - indexed cost of the shares (i.e. cos
    plus indexation allowance).
- The pool cost and the indexed cost wil
  be provided in the examination.
- When shares are disposed of out of th
  share pool, the appropriate proportion
  of the cost and indexed cost which
  relates to the shares disposed of is
  calculated on an average cost basis (a
  for individuals).

Capital allowances

The changes to the capital allowances regime for unincorporated businesses apply equally to companies, with the following additional points:

(1) The AIA must be split between related companies.

Companies owned by the same individual will be regarded as related where they:

- are engaged in the same activities,
- or share the same premises.

In such circumstances the owner of the companies can choose how to allocate a single AIA between them.

This could be the case if an individual runs two companies from home, the AIA will be split between the two businesses.

Unrelated companies owned by the same individual will each be entitled to the full AIA.

(2) For capital allowance purposes, only one AIA is available to a group of companies.

Note that:

- A 'group' for this purpose is defined by the Companies Act and essentially applies where a parent company holds a simple majority shareholding (> 50%) in another company or companies at the end of the accounting period.

When allocating the AIA:

- the group members can allocate the maximum £200,000 AIA in any way across the group
- the AIA does not have to be divided equally between them

- all of the allowance can be given to one company, or any amount can be given to any number of companies within the group.

Exam focus

Exam kit questions on this area:

Section B questions

- Sank Ltd and Kurt Ltd

(3) The 8% special rate of WDA in respect of plant and machinery that is integral to a building applies to both initial and replacement expenditure.

Replacement expenditure occurs where more than 50% of an asset is replaced a 12-month period.

This prevents a tax deduction being claimed for the repair of such assets where such repairs are substantial and the asset can be used in the trade.

Previously, a deduction was allowed for repairs expenditure, on an asset if it could be used in the trade before the 'repairs' were carried out.

This deduction is no longer available for plant and machinery integral to a building; instead tax relief is spread via the special rate WDA.

(4) Expenditure on energy saving or environmentally beneficial plant and machinery qualifies for a 100% FYA.

Where a company has made a loss:

- it may surrender that part of the loss that relates to such allowances in exchange for a payment from HMRC

- payment = loss surrendered × 2/3 CT rate (currently 12.67%).

Such a claim can only be made where the company is unable to use the losses in the current accounting period against:

- its own profits, or

- via group relief.

The claim is made in the company's corporation tax return.

The maximum payment that a company can claim is the higher of:

- £250,000 and

- its total PAYE and NIC liabilities for the relevant accounting period.

Where any of the qualifying plant and machinery is sold within four years of the end of the relevant accounting period:

- there will be a claw-back of an appropriate part of the payment made, and

- a reinstatement of the loss.

Long period of account

Accounting period > 12 months must be split into two CAPs:

- First 12 months
- Remainder

For each CAP, HMRC require:

- a separate CT comp, and
- a separate CT600 return.

Note there will be:

- Two separate pay days
  (i.e. 9 months after end of CAP)
- But only one file date of the returns
  (i.e. 12 months after end of long period of account).

Splitting the profits:

Tax adjusted trading profit before capital allowances	Time-apportion
Capital allowances	Separate computations (where the CA is less than 12 months, the WDA/AIA is reduced accordingly but not FYA)
Interest/Property/Other income	Calculate accrued amount for each period separately (Note)
Chargeable gains	According to date of disposal
Qualifying charitable donations	According to date paid

Note: if information to apply the strict accruals basis is not available, then time apportion.

Self-assessment

Payment date • Normal date • Large company (see below)	• 9 months after end of CAP • 4 quarterly instalments: on 14th of months 7, 10, 13 and 16 after start of CAP • Based on estimated liability for the year • Payments must be reviewed and revised as necessary at each instalment date. • A company will not be required to make quarterly instalments in two circumstances: (1) CT liability < £10,000 (2) Company not large in previous CAP, and augmented profits ≤ £10 million (÷ number of related 51% group companies and/or reduced for short CAP)
Payment method	• Payment must be made electronically
Filing date	• 12 months after end of period of account • Must be filed electronically along with copies of accounts • Must be filed using Inline eXtensible Business Reporting Language (iXBRL)

Late payment interest Repayment interest	• Charged from due date • Earned from date paid • Charges and receipts are interest income/expense under the loan relationship rules
Retention of records	• 6 years from end of CAP
Group payment arrangements	• Optional • Where at least one group company pays instalments • Related 51% group companies can arrange for one group company to pay quarterly instalments on behalf of group • Can save interest as overpayments effectively netted off against underpayments • Each company must still prepare separate corporation tax computation at end of CAP

Large companies

- Large companies must pay corporation tax by instalments (see table above).

- A company is large if its augmented profits for the CAP > £1.5 million threshold:

  - short CAP – time apportion threshold

  - related 51% group companies – divide by total number of related companies at end of previous CAP.

Augmented profits

	£
TTP	X
Dividends received	X
	___
Augmented profits	X
	___

- Exclude dividends from 51% group companies

Exam kit questions on this area:

Section B questions

- Sank Ltd and Kurt Ltd
- Set Ltd Group

Compliance checks

- HMRC must give written notice of their intention to commence a compliance check (enquiry) into a tax return.

- The time limit to make a compliance check:

  Where a return is submitted on time:

  - 12 months after the actual submission date.

  Where a return is submitted late:

  - 12 months after 31 January, 30 April, 31 July or 31 October following the actual filing date of the return.

- A compliance check ends when HMRC give notice.

- Company has 30 days to amend the return, if applicable.

Exam kit questions on this area:

Section B questions

- Sank Ltd and Kurt Ltd

Amendments, errors and mistakes

- A company may amend its return:
  - within 12 months from the filing date.
- HMRC may amend a return:
  - within 9 months from the date the return is filed.
- A company may make a claim for overpayment relief:
  - within four years from the end of the relevant accounting period.

Penalties

Standard penalties

- Same rules for income tax, corporation tax, CGT, VAT and NIC (see Chapter 11).

Other penalties for corporation tax

Offence	Penalty
Failure to keep and retain required records.	Up to £3,000 per accounting period.
Late filing of corporation tax return: • Within 3 months of filing date • More than 3 months after filing date Additional penalties: • 6-12 months after filing date • More than 12 months after filing date	• Fixed penalty = £100 (Note) • Fixed penalty increased to £200 (Note) • Additonal 10% of tax outstanding 6 months after filing date • Additonal penalty increased to 20% Note: Fixed penalties rise to £500 and £1,000 if persistently filed late (i.e. return for 2 preceding periods also late)

Trading losses – single company

Summary of reliefs

Carry forward relief	Current year relief	Carry back relief
		Current year offset first then carry back 12 months

• Offset against:
  – Total profits (income and gains)
  – Before QCD relief
• Optional claim
• Partial claims possible
• Indefinite carry forward
	• Offset against
	  – Total profits (income and gains)
	  – Before QCD relief
	• Carry forward any remaining losses
	• Must offset maximum amount possible if claimed
	• QCD relief is lost if no profits to offset against
	• Optional claim	

Trading loss pro forma

	2017	2018	2019
	£	£	£
Trading profit	X	0	X
Other income	X	X	X
Net chargeable gains	X	X	X
Total profits	X	X	X
Less: Loss relief			
– Current year		(X)1	
– Carry back	(X)2		
– Carry forward			(X)3
	0	0	X
Less: QCD relief	Wasted	Wasted	(X)
Taxable total profits	0	0	X

Key Point

2018 is the loss-making year. The trading profit assessment in this year is nil.

Keep a separate working of the loss and how it is utilised.

Assuming there is sufficient loss available, and assuming that the loss is being relieved as early as possible, the order in which to off-set the loss is as follows:

(1) Current year relief; in the year the loss is made.

(2) Prior year relief; carrying available losses for offset back 12 months.

(3) Future year relief; against total profits with no need to waste QCDs.

Exam focus

Use the loss pro forma to help you adopt a methodical approach to a question involving trading losses.

Show your workings in a loss working summarising how the loss has been offset.

Approach to loss offset

(1) Lay out years – columnar form.

(2) Calculate TTP ignoring losses.

(3) Choose loss relief by reference to:

- tax saving:
  - aim to save tax at highest possible rate
  - offset in FY2016 saves 20%, offset in FY2017 and future only saves 19%
- cash flow:
  - carry back may result in a repayment of tax
  - carry forward will only result in a reduction of future tax
- offet as soon as possible
- wastage of QCDs:
  - unrelieved QCDs cannot be carried foward.

(4) Use separate loss working.

(5) If more than one loss, deal with earliest first.

Exam focus

Exam kit questions on this area:

Section A questions

- Drench, Hail Ltd and Rain Ltd
- Janus plc Group
- Bond Ltd

Terminal loss relief

- Loss in final 12 months of trading
    - current year offset; then
    - carryback against total profits (before QCD relief)
    - of 3 years preceding loss making period
    - on a LIFO basis.

Exam focus

Exam kit questions on this area:

Section B questions

- Acryl Ltd and Cresco Ltd

Restriction of carry forward of losses

- Where the trade becomes small or negligible losses can only be carried forward against trading profits arising from the same trade.
- If the trade ceases losses cannot be carried forward.
- Cannot carry forward losses beyond the date of a change in ownership (> 50% shares) where:
    - a negligible trading activity is revived after a change in ownership, or
    - change in ownership and a major change in the nature of trade in a 5 year period.

Exam focus

Exam kit questions on this area:

Section B questions

- Maria and Granada Ltd

Non-trading losses

NON-TRADING LOSSES

CAPITAL LOSSES

- Current year then carry forward
- Against chargeable gains only

- Partial claims are not allowed
- Losses must be offset as soon as possible

PROPERTY INCOME LOSSES

- Current year then carry forward
- Against total profits before QCD relief

- Partial claims only allowed for losses carried forward

LOAN RELATIONSHIP DEFICITS

Four options available:

- against total profits before QCD relief of the current period
- carry back against interest income of the previous 12 months (36 months if the company is ceasing to trade)
- carry forward against total profits before QCD relief of future periods
- group relief

- Partial claims are allowed
- The company can therefore choose how much of the deficit is relieved under each option
- Claims for current period and carry back relief must be made within two years of the end of the AP of loss

Groups – corporation tax and value added tax

In this chapter

- Group relationships.
- Group relief.
- Consortium relief.
- Capital gains groups.
- Sales of shares or assets.
- Transfer of trade within 75% group.
- Transfer pricing.
- VAT group registration.

Exam focus

Questions on groups can be examined in the A or B section of the paper.

There has been a large corporation tax groups scenario on almost every ATX examination so far.

Group relationships

Relationship	Definition
Related 51% group companies	• One company directly or indirectly owns > 50% of another, or • Both are 51% subsidiaries of a third company.
Group relief (GR) group	• A parent company and all its direct and indirect 75% subsidiaries (see below). • The definition of 75% subsidiary is extended for GR purposes only. In addition to owning 75% of the share capital (SC) the parent must also be entitled to receive 75% of profits and 75% of assets on winding up.
Capital gains group	• A parent company (principal member (PM)) and its 75% subsidiaries (see below) and their 75% subsidiaries – provided PM has ⩾ 50% effective interest in subsidiary. • A 75% subsidiary of a PM cannot be a PM itself (i.e. a company can only be a member of one gains group).
75% subsidiary	• One company owns ⩾ 75% of SC of another, or • Both are 75% subsidiaries of a third company. • Includes direct/indirect holdings. • Definition includes overseas companies.

Relationship	Definition
Consortium owned company	• ≥ 75% ordinary SC owned by companies, each owning ≥ 5% and • Each member entitled to ≥ 5% profits and ≥ 5% net assets • Excludes a company that is 75% subsidiary of another.

Illustration – Group relationships

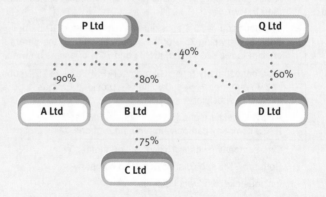

Relationship	Group members
Related 51% group companies of P Ltd	• A Ltd, B Ltd and C Ltd • D Ltd excluded as < 50%
Group relief (GR) group	• P Ltd, A Ltd, B Ltd • C Ltd is not part of the group as P Ltd's interest is < 75% i.e. interest in C Ltd = 60% (80% × 75%) • B Ltd and C Ltd form a separate losses group
Capital gains group	• P Ltd, A Ltd, B Ltd and C Ltd • C Ltd is part of the gains group as it is a 75% subsidiary of a 75% subsidiary and P Ltd's effective interest (60%) is > 50%
Consortium relief group	• D Ltd is a consortium company of P Ltd and Q Ltd • D Ltd is owned ⩾ 75% by companies and each consortium member (P Ltd and Q Ltd) is entitled to ⩾ 5%

Key Point

You must be clear on the distinction between a group relief group and a capital gains group.

- Related 51% group companies include:
  - Both UK and overseas resident companies
  - Companies leaving group.
- Exclude:
  - Dormant companies (if dormant for whole CAP)
  - Non-trading holding company
  - Companies joining the group.
- The number of related companies is based on the position at the end of the previous CAP, hence the treatment of companies joining/leaving in the period.

Effect of related 51% group companies:

Effect:

- Divide the threshold by the number of related companies to determine whether instalments are necessary.
- Dividends from related companies (UK and overseas) = not included in augmented profit.
- One AIA allocated between group companies.
- VAT group registration available.
- Group payment arrangement available if at least one company pays by quarterly instalments.

Group relief (GR)

- Transfer losses between any member of a GR group.
- Group definition:
  - includes overseas companies
  - but the relief can only be claimed by UK resident companies.

Exam focus

Exam kit questions on this area:

Section A questions

- Janus plc Group
- Drench, Hail Ltd and Rain Ltd
- Sprint Ltd and Iron Ltd
- Hahn Ltd Group
- Harrow Tan Ltd
- Set Ltd Group

Section B questions

- Cinnabar Ltd

- Rules:

Surrendering co.	Claimant co.

• **Any amount** of **current year**:
  – trading loss
  – debits on non trading loan relationships,
 	
  plus **excess**:
  – QCD relief
  – UK property losses
  – expenses of management.
 	
Can surrender **brought forward**:
  – trading losses
  – NTLR deficits
  – UK property losses
  – expenses of management.
 	
The surrendering company can only surrender to the extent it cannot use the above against its own total profits.
	Maximum claim: £
	TTP (a) X
	Less: CY losses (b) (X)
	                     X
	
	(a) TTP is after deduction of losses b/f and QCD's.
	
	(b) The company's own losses are taken into account in computing the maximum claim, but need not actually be claimed before GR.

- Watch for:
  - non-coterminous CAPs
    - GR restricted to common CAP (profits/losses deemed to accrue evenly).
  - companies joining group
    - GR only available for losses arising whilst in the group
    - Losses arising in a subsidiary before it joins the group are not available for group relief for 5 years after joining.
  - companies leaving group
    - GR only available for losses arising whilst in group, but
    - No GR once arrangements for sale are in place.

Due date for group relief claim

- 12 months after the claimant company's filing date for the CAP covered by the claim (i.e. usually 2 years after the end of the CAP).

Payment for group relief

- The claimant company may pay the surrendering company for the loss.
- Any such payment for the group relief is ignored in both companies' CT computations.

Consortium relief

- Two or more companies owning:
  - Together ≥ 75% or another company and
  - Individually ≥ 5%
  - No one company owns ≥ 75%
  - UK companies only, but overseas companies can help to meet the definition.
- Similar to group relief but:
  - Losses to surrender:
    - between consortium company (CC) and UK members only (i.e. not between members) = lower of:
      - member's TTP / trading loss
      - (member's % holding in CC) × CC's TTP / trading loss.

Exam focus

Always consider whether or not any of the companies in the question form a consortium

Exam focus

Exam kit questions on this area:

Section A questions

- Janus plc Group

Section B questions

- Cinnabar Ltd

Capital gains groups

1 Transfer of assets within group

- Automatically take place at no gain/no loss (NG/NL) regardless of the price paid.

- Transferee company takes over asset at cost plus indexation to date of transfer.

- Degrouping charge where transferee company leaves the gains group still owning the asset, within 6 years of the NG/NL transfer

  - calculated as gain that would have arisen, using MV as proceeds, at date of NG/NL transfer

  - degrouping charge is added to the consideration received by the vendor company selling the shares in the company leaving the group

  - unlikely to be taxable as company selling the shares is likely to benefit from substantial shareholding exemption on disposal of the shares

  - group ROR not available for a degrouping gain.

Exam focus

Exam kit questions on this area:

Section A questions

- Drench, Hail Ltd and Rain Ltd
- Janus plc Group
- Helm Ltd Group
- Gail
- Harrow Tan Ltd

2 Reallocation of gains

- A joint election can be made to reallocate chargeable gains or allowable losses when an asset is sold outside the group.

- The election enables:
  - group chargeable gains and allowable capital losses to be offset
  - thus maximising the use of capital losses.

Key Point

Current year chargeable gains or allowable losses can be transferred, but not brought forward losses.

3 Rollover relief (replacement of business assets)

- For ROR purposes, all companies within a capital gains group are treated as carrying on a single trade
  - gain in one company can be rolled into the acquisition by another group company
  - group ROR not available for a degrouping gain.

Exam focus

Exam kit questions on this area:

Section A questions
- Harrow Tan Ltd
- Sprint Ltd and Iron Ltd
- Bond Ltd
- Helm Ltd Group
- Hahn Ltd Group
- Heyer Ltd Group

Section B questions
- Liza

4 Pre-entry capital losses

- On joining a gains group
  - identify capital losses (realised losses only).
- Can only use against:
  - gains on own assets held at date of joining group
  - gains on new assets acquired from outside group for use in business.
- Can not be used against gains of other group companies.

5 Restriction on trading losses carried forward

If a company joins a gains group and:

- receives a gain from the new group, or
- makes a gain on an asset transferred from the new group
- within five years of changing owners

then any trading loss arising before it joined the group cannot be used against this gain.

6 Intangible assets

- Similar rules exist for transfer of intangible assets between group members (i.e. tax neutral).
- Degrouping charge if transferee company leaves group within 6 years.
- Degrouping charge can be allocated to another group member.

7 Stamp taxes

- Assets subject to stamp duty and stamp duty land tax can be transferred between group members as an exempt transfer.
- If the transferee company leaves the group within 3 years the duty is payable.

Approach to a groups question

- AIM = to allocate gains and all losses for the benefit of the group.
- The approach (as a general rule) should be as follows:
    - (i) Prepare a diagram of the group structure.
    - (ii) Determine the number of 51% group companies, 75% group(s) and consortia.
    - (iii) Set up a tabular pro forma for TTP and augmented profits (if relevant). May need to calculate gains, consider ROR and reallocation of gains to calculate TTP.
    Do this **before** dealing with losses.
    - (iv) Complete to TTP, separating out any losses to loss memoranda.
    - (v) Determine the best use of any qualifying losses to save tax as soon as possible.

- (vi) Where there are a number of losses in a question, deal with the losses with the most restricted set off first.
- (vii) Calculate CT liability on revised TTP
- (viii) Show CT payable and any losses surpluses to be carried forward.

- Also consider alternatives:
    - carrying back (after current period relief) as an alternative to GR, as this can generate a repayment, and possibly save tax at a higher rate, and
    - try to reduce the TTP of companies exceeding the threshold; this will be beneficial to the group cash flow as CT instalments will no longer be required.

Sale of shares or assets

Sale of shares:

X Ltd

- Gain/loss on disposal of shares unless SSE available.
- Possible degrouping charge: add to disposal proceeds for sale of shares.
- Still include Y Ltd as a 51% group company as it is based on the previous CAP.

Y Ltd

- Carries on trading.
- Group relief stops when arrangements in place: time apportion if mid-year.
- Trading losses c/f may be subject to restriction as Y Ltd has changed owners.
- Pre entry capital losses cannot be used against gains on Z Ltd's assets.
- Related to X Ltd until the next CAP.

Z Ltd

- Related to Y Ltd from the next CAP.
- Group relief starts when Y Ltd joins: time apportion if mid-year.
- Pay stamp duty 0.5%

Exam focus

Exam kit questions on this area:

Section A questions

- Helm Ltd Group

Sale of assets:

Before

X Ltd

100% — Y Ltd sells assets and trade to Z Ltd

Y Ltd

L&B P&M Goodwill

After

Z Ltd

L&B P&M Goodwill

X Ltd

- No effect.

Y Ltd

- Ceases trading: end of CAP.
- Gains/losses on disposal of chargeable assets (e.g. land and buildings).
- Trading profit/loss on disposal of goodwill.
- Possible ROR for gains/profit on goodwill.
- BA/BC on plant and machinery.
- Losses remain in Y Ltd: possible termina loss relief.
- VAT: transfer of going concern.

Z Ltd

- Acquires assets at MV.
- Capital allowances for plant and machinery based on MV.
- Pay stamp duty on land and buildings 0 – 5%.

Transfer of trade within a 75% group

Transfer pricing

- Applies where transactions between group companies, which have not taken place at an arms length price, result in a tax advantage (e.g. decreased profits, increased losses) to a UK company.

- The advantaged company must increase its taxable profits to reflect an arm's length price.

- The other company can reduce its taxable profits by a corresponding amount if it is UK resident.

- Rules only apply where the companies involved are large (or medium sized under limited circumstances).

- Rules do apply if:

  Large → any company
  S/M → overseas company in non-qualifying territory
  (e.g. no DTR agreement).

- Rules do not apply if:

  S/M → UK S/M

  S/M → overseas company in qualifying territory
  (e.g. DTR agreement exists).

VAT Group registration

- Membership
  - voluntary
  - by any UK companies under common control.
- Consequences
  - Representative member responsible for accounting for VAT
  - No VAT on intra-group sales
  - Only one VAT return to prepare
  - All members jointly/severally liable for group VAT
  - Limits for cash accounting scheme applied to whole group
  - Other VAT schemes for small businesses not available.

Be prepared to explain whether or not a company should be included in a VAT group.

- Special consideration required for:
  - company making zero rated supplies
    - exclude if in monthly repayment position to maintain cash flow advantage
  - companies making exempt supplies
    - inclusion in group will make the group partially exempt.

Exam focus

Exam kit questions on this area:

Section A questions

- Sprint Ltd and Iron Ltd
- Hahn Ltd Group

Section B questions

- Liza

17

Overseas issues – corporation tax and value added tax

In this chapter

- Company residence.
- UK company operating overseas.
- Branch exemption election.
- Overseas income – computational approach.
- Controlled foreign companies.
- Overseas aspects of VAT.

Exam focus

Overseas issues are likely to feature as part of a question and are often included within a groups question.

Company residence

Definition

A company is resident in the UK if it is:

- **incorporated** in the UK, or
- incorporated outside the UK and
  - its place of **central management and control** is situated in the UK.

Exam focus

Exam kit questions on this area:

Section B questions

- Spetz Ltd Group

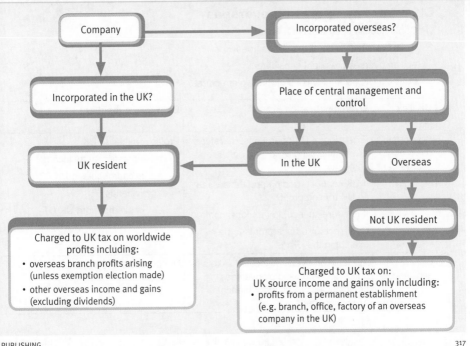

UK company operating overseas

- Can establish operations in 2 ways:
  - a branch/division of the UK company, or
  - an overseas resident subsidiary.
- Different UK tax implications of the two structures.

UK Tax factor	Overseas branch	Overseas subsidiary

Scope and basis of charge	Extension of UK operations; therefore all profits arising assessed on UK company.
	
	If UK control – trading profit assessed as UK trading profit.
	
	If not, foreign income (i.e. local control).
	
	Can elect for branch profits to be exempt in the UK.
		Profits remitted to UK
		• as interest/property income:
		  – is chargeable to UK CT
		• as dividends:
		  – is exempt from UK CT

Capital allowances	Available on overseas located assets purchased and used by overseas branch unless election for branch exemption made.	Not available under UK tax rules.

UK Tax factor (contd)	Overseas branch (contd)	Overseas subsidiary (contd)
Trading loss relief	Can relieve trading losses against UK profits. No relief if election for branch exemption made. Can use UK losses against profits of overseas branch.	No UK trading loss can be surrendered to overseas subsidiary.
Chargeable gains	Capital gains computed using UK rules (i.e. ROR is available on reinvestment and capital losses can be utilised).	UK rules not applicable.
Impact on tax payment dates	None – as **not** a separate entity.	51% group company: • Reduces the threshold for determining whether instalments are required. • If dividend received from overseas 51% group company = ignored for augmented profits. • If dividend received from overseas non 51% group = included in augmented profits.

Exam focus

Exam kit questions on this area:

Section B questions

- Spetz Ltd Group

Branch exemption election

- Can be made at any time
- Effective from start of CAP after election made
- Irrevocable
- Applies to all overseas branches

Effect

- Profits = exempt in UK
- Losses = no relief in UK
- No capital allowances
- Capital gains = not taxable in UK

Tax planning

- May be beneficial not to make election if:
    (i) DTR means little or no UK CT payable, and/or
    (ii) losses possible or anticipated in an overseas branch in the future.

Overseas income – computational approach

(1) Calculate the gross amount of overseas income for inclusion in computation of TTP.

	£
Foreign income received	A
Add: WHT = A × $\frac{\% \text{ WHT}}{100 - \% \text{WHT}}$	X
	X

(2) Compute the CT liability on the TTP.

(3) Offset DTR

For each source of overseas income lower of:

– overseas tax suffered, and

– UK tax on overseas income.

(4) Unrelieved overseas tax on branch profits only

Relief may be available via:

– carry back

– carry forward.

Key Point

Offset QCD relief and losses against UK income to maximise DTR.

Exam focus

Exam kit questions on this area:

Section B questions

- Banger Ltd and Candle Ltd

- Spetz Ltd Group

Controlled foreign companies (CFCs)

Exam focus

Always consider the possibility of an overseas company being a CFC

- Provisions exist to prevent UK companies setting up overseas subsidiaries and accumulating profits in countries with lower rates of tax.

Definition

A non-UK resident company:

- Controlled by UK resident companies, and/or individuals
- that has artificially diverted profits from the UK.

Key Point

The usual rule of taxing only non-dividend income from an overseas subsidiary and exempting dividend income does not apply to a CFC.

CFC charge to UK corporation tax

- A CFC charge applies if:

  - **UK company owns ≥ 25%** interest in the CFC

  - the CFC has chargeable profits.

- CFC charge is:

	£
(UK company's share of CFC profits x 19% of CT) (see Note)	X
Less: Creditable tax	
DTR that would be available if CFC were UK resident	(X)
UK CT on income of CFC that is taxable in UK (if any)	(X)
Income tax suffered by the CFC on its income (if any)	(X)
CFC charge	X

Note: UK company's share of CFC profits

> = **apportioned based on the % of shares held**

- UK companies self assess their liability to the CFC charge.

- A clearance procedure exists to check how the rules will be applied.

No CFC charge

- CFC charge does not arise if
  - no chargeable profits of CFC
  - an exemption applies
  - the shareholder = an individual.

No chargeable profits of CFC

- **Chargeable profits** = income of CFC (not chargeable gains) that are artificiall diverted from the UK, calculated using the UK tax rules.
- CFCs = regarded as having **no chargeable profits** (and therefore no CFC charge) if:
  - the CFC does not hold assets or bear any risks
    - that are managed in the UK, or are
    - under tax schemes intended to reduce UK tax, or
  - the CFC would continue in business if the UK management of its assets and risks were to cease.

Exemptions to CFC charge

- CFC may have chargeable profits, but no CFC charge as it satisfies one of the exemptions:

Exempt period	The first 12 months of the company coming under the control of UK residents.
Excluded territories	HMRC provide a list of approved territories where rates of tax are sufficiently high to avoid a CFC charge arising.
Low profits	The CFC's TTPs are: • ≤ £500,000 in a 12-month period – of which ≤ £50,000 comprises non-trading profits.
Low profit margin	The CFC's accounting profits are ≤ 10% of relevant operating expenditure.
Tax exemption	The tax paid in the overseas country is ≥ 75% of the UK CT which would be due if it were a UK resident company.

Exam focus

Exam kit questions on this area:

Section A questions

- Set Ltd Group

Section B questions

- Klubb plc

Overseas aspects of VAT

EU transactions for supply of goods

	'Destination system'	'Origin system'
Status of parties	Supplier and customer VAT registered (Business to business) (B2B)	Supplier registered, customer not registered (Business to individual) (B2C)
Rate of VAT	Country of origin • zero rated Destination country • rate applicable in destination country	Country of origin • rate applicable in country of origin
Supplier	No VAT	Account for output tax May have to register in country of destination if supplies exceed threshold
Customer	Pays output VAT based on date of acquisition, which is the earlier of: • date of invoice • 15th day of month following month goods came into UK Claims VAT suffered as input tax	Cannot recover VAT as not registered

Non-EU transactions for supply of goods

Imports

- Importer pays VAT at point of entry into UK.
- Can pay monthly through Duty Deferment System.
- Recovers VAT suffered as input tax.
- Net effect is the same as for purchases from the UK.

Exports

- All goods are zero rated.

Key Point

All supplies of goods within or outside the EU = taxable supplies.

Issue = whether the supply is zero or standard rated.

It will never be an exempt supply.

Net effect on purchases from within or outside the EU = same, unless purchaser makes exempt supplies.

Supply of services

VAT is generally charged in the place of supply.

Supply of services to	Place of supply
Business customer	Where the customer is established
Non-business customer	Where the supplier is established

These rules can be applied to a UK business as follows:

UK business		Accounting for VAT
Supplies services to	• Overseas business customer (B2B)	• Place of supply is overseas. • Outside the scope of UK VAT.
	• Overseas non-business customer (B2C)	• Place of supply is UK. • Output VAT charged at standard UK rate.

Receives services from	• Overseas business (B2B)	• Place of supply is UK.
		• Reverse charge procedure:
		  – UK business accounts for 'output VAT' at standard UK rate on VAT return.
		  – This VAT can then be reclaimed as input VAT.

Time of supply for cross border supply of services

- For single supplies:
  - tax point = earlier of
    - (i) when the service is completed, or
    - (ii) paid for
- For continuous supplies:
  - tax point = end of each billing or payment period

Exam focus

Exam kit questions on this area:

Section A questions
- Janus plc Group
- Set Ltd Group

Section B questions
- Meg and Laurie

Business finance and tax planning for companies

In this chapter

- Long term finance.
- Short term finance.
- Financing non-current assets.
- Business vehicle.
- Extracting profits from a business.
- Incorporation of a business.
- Close companies.
- Personal service company.
- Withdrawing investment.
- Tax planning for companies.

Long term finance

Debt versus Equity

	Equity	Debt
Maximum amount	• Specified in Articles of Association	• No limit
Return on investment	• Dividends • Only paid if profitable	• Interest • Paid regardless of profitability
Corporate investors	• Dividends received = exempt	• Interest received = taxable
Individual investors	• Basic rate and higher rate taxpayers have savings nil rate bands available • All taxpayers have a £2,000 dividend nil rate band. Amounts in excess of this will be taxed at 7.5%/32.5%/38.1% depending on the taxpayers level of income	

Other points	• If not listed:
	  – difficult to issue new shares
	• Owner managed businesses:
	  – may not like control to be diluted
	  – usually issue shares to existing shareholders or family members
		• lender may require security (i.e. a charge over company assets)

Incentives to issue shares

For individuals:

- SEIS relief.
- EIS relief.
- VCT relief.

For companies:

- Substantial shareholding exemption.

Short term finance

- Bank overdraft.
- Short term loans.
- Trade credit.
- Invoice discounting.
- Debt factoring.
- Hire purchase and leasing.

Financing non-current assets

	Outright purchase	Hire purchase	Leasing
Initial outlay	• Full cost	• Instalment	• Lease rental
Subsequent cost of purchase	• None	• Instalments spread over length of HP agreement • Includes HP interest	• Lease rentals spread over length of lease • Includes finance charge
Tax relief against profit	• Capital allowances available	• Interest = allowable deduction against profit • Capital allowances available	• Lease rental and depreciation = allowable deduction against profit (other than high emission cars with $CO_2 > 110$ g/km where 15% of lease charge is disallowed) • No capital allowances
VAT recoverable? (except cars)	Yes	Yes	Yes
Sale proceeds on disposal	Yes	Yes	No

Business vehicle

Sole trader versus company

	Sole trader	Company
Taxation of profits	• Current year basis	• Accounting period basis
	• Assessed to income tax	• Assessed to corporation tax
	• Based on taxable trading profits	• Based on taxable total profits
	• Adjustments for private use	• Taxable total profits = after individual's employment income deducted
	• Personal allowance may be available	
	• Taxed at 20%, 40% or 45%	• No adjustments for private use
	• Class 2 NICs	• No personal allowance
	• Class 4 NICs	• Taxed at 19%
		• No NICs on business profits
		• Individual assessed to income tax and class 1 NICs on employment income

	Sole trader (contd)	Company (contd)
Relief for losses	• Available against personal income of individual • Against total income of current and/or previous tax year • Extension claim against chargeable gains in same years • Opening year relief against total income of previous 3 tax years, FIFO basis • Carry forward relief against trading profits of same trade	• Available against company profits only • Against total profits (income and gains) of current year • Carry back 12 months • Carry forward against total profits

Withdrawal of funds	• No tax implications	• Salary/bonus versus dividend (see below)
		
		• Alternatives:
		
		  – Rent (but could affect eligibility to ER)
		
		  – Pension contributions

VAT	• Individual registers	• Company registers

	Sole trader (contd)	Company (contd)

Disposal of business interest	• Disposal of unincorporated business = gains on individual chargeable assets
	• Entrepreneurs' relief for CGT
	• If gifted:
	  – Gift relief available for CGT
	  – BPR available for IHT
	• If incorporated:
	  – Incorporation relief or
	  – Gift relief for CGT
		• Disposal of shares
		• Entrepreneurs' relief
		• If gifted:
		  – Gift relief for CGT may be available
		  – BPR for IHT may be available

Key Point

Where initial losses are anticipated, order events to ensure losses can be relieved against the individuals income and then incorporate business when it becomes profitable.

Extracting profits from a business

	Additional salary (i.e. bonus)	Dividend
Rates of income tax	IT liability = IT payable = 20%, 40% or 45%	IT liability = 7.5%, 32.5% or 38.1% of dividend
NICs paid by individual	Employee class 1 at 12% or 2%	No NICs payable
NICs paid by company	Employer's class 1 at 13.8%	No NICs payable
Corporation tax implications	Salary and Employer's class 1 NICs = allowable deductions for corporation tax	None
Pension contributions	Salary = relevant earnings for pension relief purposes	Dividends = not relevant earnings for pension relief purposes

 Exam focus

Exam kit questions on this area:

Section A questions

- Gail
- Florina, Kanzi and Winston

Section B questions

- Bamburg Ltd
- Traiste Ltd

Disposal of interest in an unincorporated business

	Income tax	CGT	IHT
Sale of business	• Last adjustment of profits • Last capital allowances • BCs and BAs • Closing year rules applied	• Gains arise on every single chargeable asset • ROR • Entrepreneurs' relief	• No diminution in value • No IHT
Lifetime gift of business	As above	• Gains arise on every single chargeable asset • Gift relief • Entrepreneurs' relief	• PET or CLT • BPR = 100% Also available on death provided donee still owns business when donor dies
Death owning business	As above	• No CGT on death	• Business included in Death estate • BPR = 100%

Incorporation of a business

Incorporation is a popular area for examination questions as it can test knowledge of all taxes in the syllabus:

- Income tax
- Corporation tax
- National insurance
- VAT
- SDLT
- Inheritance tax
- Capital gains tax

Exam kit questions on this area:

Section A questions

- Farina and Lauda
- Waverley

Section B questions

- Jerome and Tricycle Ltd

Income tax
- Formerly profits of trade assessed to income tax
- Drawings and private use = not allowable deductions against profit
- Closing year rules apply on incorporation
- Balancing adjustments arise unless succession election applies
- If loss making Incorporation relief available (Chapter 13)

NICs
- Formerly liable to class 2 and class 4 NICs
- Now liable to employee class 1
- Company liable to employer's class 1 and class 1 A NICs

Value Added Tax
Not a taxable supply
Provided conditions satisfied (Chapter 14)

Corporation tax
- Profits of trade now assessed to corporation tax
- Individual becomes director/shareholder
- Individual assessed to employment income and dividends
- Employment income and employers NICs = allowable deductions against profit

Incorporation

Capital gains tax
- Disposal of individual assets
- Incorporation relief or gift relief available (Chapter 6)

Inheritance tax
- No transfer of value
- No diminution in value

Stamp duty land tax
Payable by the company on purchase of land and buildings

Close companies

Close company = a company with close proprietorial control

(i.e. controlled by five or fewer shareholders or any number of directors usually a family company, an owner managed business)

1 Benefits provided to shareholders who are not employees

Shareholder	Close company
If shareholder = not an employee • Individual = treated as receiving a dividend • subject to income tax at 7.5%, 32.5% or 38.1% • Value of the deemed cash dividend = the benefit which would have been assessable if they had been an employee of the company	• Company = treated as paying a dividend to the shareholder • Costs of providing benefit = not allowable for the company • No class 1A NICs on deemed dividend
If shareholder = an employee • Individual = treated as receiving a normal benefit of employment	• Company = treated as giving a normal benefit to an employee • Costs of providing benefit = allowable for the company • Class 1A NICs payable

2 Loans provided to shareholders

Shareholder	Close company

• If loan is granted with a beneficial rate of interest, the loan benefit assessed as a beneficial loan (see benefits above).
 	
• If the loan is written off by the company, the individual
= treated as receiving a cash dividend equivalent to the loan written off.
 	
• Subject to income tax at 7.5%, 32.5% or 38.1%.
	• Company must pay tax charge
	  = 32.5% × loan advance if still outstanding at the normal due date (i.e. 9 months after end of the accounting period).
	
	• Tax charge = payable with corporation tax.
	
	• Repaid 9 months after AP end in which
	  – loan repaid
	  – loan written off.
	
	• Tax charge does not apply if
	  1 Amount loaned ≤ £15,000
	  2 Individual = full time employee
	  3 Individual (with associates) owns < 5% interest in the company.

3 Close investment company (CIC)

- Not qualifying interest i.e. not deductible.

4 Shareholder borrows money to buy shares in a close company

- Qualifying loan interest paid

  = allowable relief in shareholder's income tax computation

- reduces taxable income of individual.

Exam focus

Exam kit questions with close company aspects:

Section A questions

- Drench, Rain Ltd and Hail Ltd

Section B questions

- Banger Ltd and Candle Ltd
- Bamburg Ltd
- Nocturne Ltd
- Methley Ltd

Personal service company

Exam kit questions on this area:

Section B questions

- Monisha and Horner
- Eric

Withdrawing investment

Withdrawing investment from a company

Sale of shares

CGT – payable

May be difficult to achieve as no ready market for unquoted shares

Purchase of own shares

Conditions satisfied:
– capital disposal liable to CGT and entrepreneurs' relief if personal trading company

Conditions not satisfied:
– treated as dividend
= amount received less nominal value of shares

Liquidation of company

Payments before liquidator appointed = income

Payments after liquidator appointed = capital

HMRC allows winding-up without a liquidator and payments to be treated as capital (max £25,000)

Purchase of own shares

Conditions for capital treatment:

(1) The company must be an unquoted trading company.

(2) Be able to demonstrate that the repurchase of the shares is for the benefit of the trade and not part of a scheme to avoid tax.

Examples of benefit to trade:

– buying out retiring directors

– buying out dissident shareholders

– shareholder has died and beneficiaries don't want shares

– venture capitalist withdrawing investment.

(3) The individual must be resident in the UK.

(4) Have owned the shares for 5 years prior to the repurchase (3 years if inherited).

(5) Reduce their shareholding substantially after the buyback – the shareholder must end up with:

– No more than 30% of the shares in the company, and

– No more than 75% of the previous percentage holding.

Exam focus

Exam kit questions with purchase of own shares:

Section B questions

• Trifles Ltd

• Traiste Ltd

Exam kit questions with liquidation:

Section B questions

• Banger Ltd and Candle Ltd

• Maria and Granada Ltd

• Acryl Ltd and Cresco Ltd

Tax planning for companies

Investments to save tax

- Capital expenditure.
- R&D expenditure.

Tax planning

- Optimum use of losses.
- Group structure.
- Maximising group corporation tax reliefs.

Index

Z